DECLARATIONS OF TRUST:
A DRAFTSMAN'S HANDBOOK

William M Hartley
MA (Cantab)

LAW & TAX

ISBN 085121 9918

Published by
FT Law & Tax
21–27 Lamb's Conduit Street
London WC1N 3NJ

A Division of Pearson Professional Limited

Associated offices
Australia, Belgium, Canada, Hong Kong, India, Japan,
Luxembourg, Singapore, Spain, USA

A CIP catalogue record for this book is available from the British
Library

Printed by Bell and Bain, Glasgow.

Contents

Precedents

Preface

Sometime in 1993, I needed to draft a declaration of trust to tidy up a messy transaction where different people had contributed different amounts for the purchase of property and wished to hold their interests in different ways. A search through the usual precedent books did not reveal the specimen I was looking for. It did, however, make me aware that perhaps there was a need for a straightforward book on declarations of trust if only to make practitioners aware of their usefulness, and it is hoped that this is it.

It is a measure of the patience of my publisher that this book only appears now. My thanks are due not only to Susan Marshall of FT Law and Tax for her encouragement in bringing this project to fruition but to my colleagues and staff who have been asked for suggestions, practical help and ideas at what must often have been inconvenient times.

The law is stated as at 1 June 1995.

June 1995   William M Hartley
Manchester

Table of Cases

Table of Statutes

Table of Statutory Instruments

1

General principles

1 Introduction

Declarations of trust are most commonly used to set out the interests of parties where an asset is held by more than one person. The parties may decide that the benefit of the assets should be held in equal shares or in some other proportion. Thus, a declaration of trust can be used when a couple set up home together or when there is a joint venture. Similarly an asset may have been purchased jointly and the parties may decide that their interests should be more specifically defined so that the property does not pass to the survivor of them on death. A declaration of trust has further value in that equitable ownership in an asset may pass to another while legal title remains where it is.

The making of a declaration of trust can often be viewed as the tidying up of the file; the main transaction is completed and the parties appear clear about what is intended when the period of the trust comes to an end. All too often the making of the declaration is put on one side. Its importance can be overlooked until there is either disagreement between the parties or with third parties, such as the Inland Revenue or a trustee in bankruptcy. It is only then that the value of the declaration comes into its own, for not only may it regulate the interests in the asset between the parties concerned but it provides evidence of entitlement.

The aim of this book is to provide some precedents so that the tidying up is made easier and is actually done, and also to provide indications as to the uses of declarations of trust. Inevitably the precedents that follow only touch on the most common situations. Before turning to the separate chapters and precedents, it might be helpful to refer to various general points, some of which can help to emphasise the role of a declaration of trust.

In these days of equality, it is important to emphasise that the masculine includes the feminine and vice versa (Interpretation Act 1978, s 6); similarly, no discrimination is intended and the precedents should be capable of adaptation, whatever the relationship of the parties.

2   The certainties of a trust

The declarations of trust contained in this book each constitute an express trust, many of them for the persons actually making the declaration. It is important to remember the three certainties necessary to constitute an express trust:

> (1) certainty of the subject matter of the trust (see *Hunter v Moss* [1994] 1 WLR 452; below p 87);
> (2) certainty of beneficiaries; and
> (3) certainty of the interests the beneficiaries are to take.

Whilst trusts of pure personalty may be constituted by oral declarations, any declaration of trust respecting land or any interest therein must be in writing signed by some person who is able to declare such trusts (Law of Property Act 1925, s 53).

However, a written declaration gives a greater chance of certainty for assets which are not land, not least because the parties have to consider what is to be contained in the declaration.

3   Presumption of advancement

An implied or resulting trust arises where, on a purchase, property is conveyed into the name of someone other than the purchaser. The result of this is that the trust of a legal estate, whether taken in the names of the purchasers and others jointly, or in the names of others without that of the purchaser, and whether in one name or several, results to the person who advances the purchase money.

The doctrine applies to personalty as well as land (*Re Scottish Equitable Life Assurance Society* [1902] 1 Ch 282). It also applies where two or more persons advance purchase money jointly and the purchase is taken in the name of one only, with the resulting trust arising in favour of the persons who advanced the money.

However, the doctrine of a resulting trust will not arise where the relationship existing between the person who advances the money and the person in whose name the asset is purchased is such as to raise a presumption that a gift was intended. The presumption of advancement arises if a husband purchases a property in the name of a wife, or a father purchases a property in the name of a child. In the absence of evidence to the contrary, the presumption of advancement would presume that a gift was to be made.

Whilst the equitable presumption of advancement is now considered a 'judicial instrument of last resort' (*Pettitt v Pettitt* [1970] AC 777) it cannot be lightly dismissed and is a clear reason, where there are transactions between parties of the relationship mentioned above, why a declaration of trust should be made.

Indeed, the recent case of *McGrath v Wallis* (1995) *The Times*, 13 April provides such an example. A father's house was sold and the proceeds utilised in the purchase of another house to be occupied by himself and his son. This other house was purchased in the son's name so as to enable mortgage finance to be obtained. On the father's death, the other son claimed that the father's interest in the property should fall into his estate. The son who held the legal title claimed otherwise, raising in his support the presumption of advancement.

The irony of this case, which was used to rebut the presumption, was that a declaration of trust had been prepared but never executed. What better example of a case where a declaration of trust should have been made to make the parties entitlements absolutely clear?

4 Insolvency

A transaction effected at an undervalue (for example a gift) can be set aside, on the application of a trustee in bankruptcy, if it took place within two years prior to the presentation of the bankruptcy petition or if it took place within five years prior to the presentation of the petition and the individual was insolvent at the time of the transaction or became insolvent because of it. The court has a discretion as to the appropriate order to make and is not necessarily required to set the transaction aside completely (Insolvency Act 1986, ss 339–342).

Thus, any declaration of trust which contains an element of gift can run the risk of being set aside (Insolvency Act 1986, s 423). However, the declaration of trust can be of real value (particularly once it is outside the time limit mentioned above) in showing to a trustee in bankruptcy the extent of the interests of both the bankrupt and the solvent co-owner. If there is no such declaration, or where property is held jointly, then the trustee may well allege that the whole of the asset should fall into the bankrupt's estate.

5   Legal title

Legal title to land can only be held by four persons (Law of Property Act 1925, s 34(2)). Where more than four people are to have an interest in land then the interests of all should be set out in a separate document, such as a declaration of trust or partnership agreement.

It is not unusual for a party to borrow money to buy his share. The lender will naturally want security by taking a charge on the underlying property (and thus from the four legal owners), and they in turn will require an indemnity from the borrowing party which can be dealt with in the declaration of trust setting out the various parties' interests.

6   Tax

Whilst this book does not set out to be a tax book, tax should never be far from the practitioner's mind when advising his client. With regard to tax, the following points should be borne in mind.

(a)   Income Tax

The declaration of trust can be particularly relevant in arranging affairs judiciously for income tax purposes where property which produces income is held by husband and wife (see further Chapter 2).

(b)   Capital Gains Tax

A declaration of trust which in effect disposes of a party's interest in an asset (whether in whole or in part) is a disposal for Capital Gains

Tax purposes. It is appropriate therefore to be aware of the exemptions and reliefs.

Spouses living together

There is no charge to Capital Gains Tax on a transfer of assets between husband and wife provided that they are living together in the year of assessment in which the transfer takes place (Taxation of Chargeable Gains Act 1992, s 58). Thus, where property is held by one party to the marriage and subsequently declared to be held for both parties, no charge to Capital Gains Tax would arise on that effective transfer.

Only or main residence

Gains accruing on the disposal of, or an interest in, a dwellinghouse which is or has been an individual's only or main residence (together with gardens or grounds of up to half a hectare in extent or other extent appropriate for the reasonable enjoyment of the residence according to the size and character of the dwellinghouse) throughout the period of ownership but disregarding the last 36 months of that period (TCGA 1992, s 223) are exempt from Capital Gains Tax (TCGA 1992, s 222). Thus, a disposal through the medium of a declaration of trust (see Chapter 4) in such a case would not incur a liability to Capital Gains Tax.

Annual exemption

There is an annual exemption of £6,000 available for each party holding an interest in a property. It is helpful to be able to prove to the Inland Revenue the extent of that interest by way of a declaration of trust.

Hold over relief

In the case of company shares remaining in the name of the registered shareholder but held for another (see Chapter 6), it should be considered whether or not hold over relief for Capital Gains Tax purposes may be available on the transfer of the interest which occurs on the making of the declaration (TCGA 1992, s 165).

Hold over relief is available where there is a disposal by an individual either by way of gift or by way of a sale at undervalue, and the relief is limited to gifts of business assets (TCGA 1992, s 165(2)). Non business assets do not attract relief and that part of the gain on a disposal of shares in a company which owns non business assets is therefore excluded from relief, a point often overlooked.

A claim for hold over relief under the section will have to be made by both transferor and transferee.

(c) Inheritance Tax

A disposal for Inheritance Tax purposes can occur on the making of a declaration of trust whereby the transferor's estate is reduced, so that it is appropriate to be aware of the exemptions and reliefs.

Potentially exempt transfer
An absolute gift to a donee is a potentially exempt transfer for Inheritance Tax purposes (Inheritance Tax Act 1984, s 3A(*i*)) and would generally therefore fall out of charge for IHT purposes if the donor survives the gift by seven years. If death occurs within the seven-year period the recipient is primarily liable for any tax referable to the gift (s 199(1)(*b*)). As the tax can be collected from the personal representatives it is not unusual for the donor to require an indemnity from the donee to pay any such tax.

Husband and wife
If both husband and wife are domiciled in the United Kingdom, any transfer of assets between them is exempt from any charge to Inheritance Tax (IHTA 1984, s 18(1)).

Nil band
The first £154,000 of a person's estate is taxed at a nil rate. It is appropriate that where a husband and wife hold a house which has valuable equity then, if held as beneficial joint tenants, the tenancy should be severed so as to ensure at the very least that in the event of common accident their respective interests go under their respective wills (thus hopefully taking advantage of the nil band in each case). To prove the extent of their interest, therefore, there should be a declaration of trust following the severance. In a non husband and wife situation where a sole owner makes a declaration of trust in favour of another then the provisions mentioned above should be considered. The main point however is that any declaration of trust is evidential as to the extent of the interests of the beneficiary concerned.

(d) Stamp Duty

Stamp duty is not usually a major consideration as far as declarations of trust are concerned, other than to utilise the declaration of trust for the purposes of avoiding a liability to stamp duty (see further at p 54).

7 Parties to the declaration

Where an individual declares that he holds an asset (or an interest in it) for another, the question may be raised as to whether or not the recipient needs to be a party to the declaration. Obviously the recipient must be a party where, for instance, he is giving an indemnity to the declarer.

It is thought to be prudent for the recipient to be a party in all cases, as not only does this confirm acceptance of the gift (if it is a gift situation), but it confirms agreement of the interests to be taken in the property which is the subject of the declaration.

8 Registered and unregistered land

Although the majority of land transactions now relate to registered land, there are still a large number of unregistered titles and it is appropriate that both types of land should be considered. Although the property concerned may be in an area subject to compulsory registration of title, no application for such registration is required when any conveyance has not been one following sale (Land Registration Act 1925, s 123).

2

Property purchased as tenants in common

1 Introduction

There are many reasons why real property purchased jointly should
be held by the purchasers as tenants in common and why the respective shares should be defined by a declaration of trust.

(a) Interest of a person entitled to a share of sale proceeds

A declaration of trust should make it clear as to the respective interests of the co-owners so that in the event of a split of co-habitees or
partners, the division of the proceeds of sale is beyond dispute. It will
be appreciated that very often a property is purchased in the names
of two persons and whilst they may hold it for themselves as tenants
in common (for instance co-habitees or two sisters), they may hold it
for several people (for instance six partners in a doctor's practice).

Where the property is a matrimonial asset other factors come into
play, although the declaration may be useful evidence as to who provided the purchase monies in the first place.

(b) Devolution on death

The share of a deceased co-owner will devolve in accordance with
his will or on intestacy or in accordance with the terms of the declaration of trust.

(c) Inheritance Tax

The declaration of trust provides evidence as to the shares of the
owners of the property.

(d)   Insolvency

In the event of the insolvency of one of the owners, the declaration provides evidence as to what percentage of the proceeds of sale belong to the bankrupt's estate.

(e)   Income Tax

It is useful to define the shares so that any rental income can be returned accordingly. It is generally assumed by the Inland Revenue that income from property held jointly by husband and wife should be split 50/50 (Income and Corporation Taxes Act 1988, s 282A). A declaration of trust provides evidence to the contrary, although notification must be given to the Revenue within 60 days on Inland Revenue Form 17 (ICTA 1988, s 282B(3)). Conversely, if no notification is given, then even if the shares are not equal, husband and wife are taxed on the 50/50 basis which could be useful in providing the wife with an income for tax purposes (at lower rate) even though the asset is owned (say) 75 per cent by the husband.

For non husband and wife, the declaration provides the appropriate evidence for a split of the income.

(f)   Capital Gains Tax

The declaration of trust evidences the ownership of the respective interests for capital gains tax purposes.

2   The legal title

It has been mentioned that the shares of joint holders of property should be defined by a declaration of trust (see above). The whole purpose of the 1925 property legislation was to keep equitable interests off the legal title and indeed the Land Registration Act 1925, s 74 provides that so far as possible, references to trusts shall be excluded from the Register.

(a)   Unregistered land

The conveyance to the parties who are to hold the property would normally declare that they hold the same 'as tenants in common in equal shares' (or as the case may be), or alternatively that it is held by them as trustees 'upon the trusts of a declaration of trust of even date to be executed immediately after this Deed'.

In practice it is often some time before a declaration is executed—the priority has been to complete the conveyance. In any event, if the division of shares is to be by reference to the total costs incurred in purchase (and not just the purchase price), the relevant figures may not be known at the time of completion. In such circumstances, the conveyance probably merely specifies that the purchasers hold the property as tenants in common (see below, p 33 if nothing further is done).

(b)   Registered land

So far as this is concerned, two or more purchasers will have to declare whether the survivor of them can or cannot give a good receipt for capital monies (see HMLR Form 19(JP)). The latter being applicable, the Registry will register a restriction to the effect that no disposition by a sole proprietor of the land (not being a trust corporation) under which capital money arises is to be registered except under an order of the Registrar or of the court. (Land Registration Act 1925, s 58(3) and Land Registration Rules 1925 (SR & O No 1093) r 213 as amended by Land Registration Rules 1989 (SI No 801)).

The parties will also have to consider whether they wish to extend the restriction, for instance to deal with consent to the appointment of a new joint proprietor in the event of the death of one of the registered proprietors by the personal representatives of the deceased joint proprietor or whether they are content to rely upon the survivor having the power of appointment of a new proprietor under the Trustee Act 1925, s 36.

3   The contents of the declaration

The precedents that follow in this chapter concentrate on the split of the proceeds of sale and the percentage interests of the parties. However, there is no reason why the declaration should not contain (if applicable) provisions as to the subjects set out below.

(a) Outgoings

It should be agreed as to whether or not a party who pays outgoings such as insurance, chief rent etc should be reimbursed. The practical view is that the occupier of the property should pay these.

(b) Repairs

It should be agreed as to whether or not one party has the obligation to see to repairs and either to pay the costs, or perhaps receive reimbursement as to half (or whatever agreed proportion) out of the proceeds of sale before division.

(c) Power of sale

Land (not being settled land) held by two or more persons is held upon trust to sell the same (Law of Property Act 1925, s 36). If, therefore, there are to be restrictions as to when a sale is to take place, these should be contained in the declaration of trust (see Precedents 9 or 10).

It will be appreciated that while such an agreement may be binding *inter partes*, it will not bind a mortgagee, who will only have been concerned with the legal estate.

(d) Mortgage payments

It should be considered who is to be responsible for paying these and whether or not there is to be any form of reimbursement on sale. Given the different forms of mortgages, this can present real difficulty and the majority of cohabitees, for instance, will accept that either the mortgage is to be paid equally, or that one of them is entitled to a greater percentage of the proceeds of sale (such percentage being fixed at the outset), given the fact that he or she is to be paying the mortgage (or most of it). This is probably preferable to keeping detailed accounts and records. However, the question of the mortgage must be thought about as should the entitlement to any life policy or PEP taken out in connection therewith.

Where property is purchased by several people, they may have effected separate borrowing arrangements. Whilst a mortgagee will take a legal charge over the property, the owners will wish to cover this position as between themselves.

It will be appreciated that an indemnity will be worthless if the party giving it has no assets or income stream to back it up.

It seems to be common practice for instance for medical practitioners to purchase premises, and obviously from time to time there are changes in the medical partnership, with a new partner often purchasing a retiring partner's share in the premises. It is usual for the same bank to finance each of the partners, taking a charge on the surgery premises to secure those borrowings. It is important, therefore, between themselves that the partners create cross-indemnities. (see Precedent 7).

Similarly, a husband may wish to borrow monies on the security of a second mortgage on the house owned by himself and his wife for the purposes of his business. Whilst they are both primarily liable to the mortgagee in respect of such mortgage, the wife may wish to protect her interest in the dwellinghouse so far as she can. She should certainly insist on the lender agreeing a limit to the amount of borrowing being charged on the property and should obtain an indemnity from the husband in respect of the second mortgage (see Precedent 5).

4   Death of a tenant in common

Where the death of a tenant in common occurs so that the legal title stands in the name of one person alone, it is necessary to appoint a further trustee of the legal estate so that a good receipt for capital monies is obtained by any purchaser (Law of Property Act 1925, s 27) and indeed, in the case of registered land, so that a transfer will be registered. (see restriction above, p 10).

The original declaration of trust may specify that the power of appointment of a new trustee on the death of one of the trustees is vested in the personal representatives of that trustee.

Subject to the provisions of the original declaration of trust the Trustee Act 1925, s 36 allows a surviving trustee to appoint a new trustee. If it is not envisaged that the property will be sold until after the death of the surviving tenant in common it might be prudent to appoint two new trustees so that they are in place at the time of the second death. (see Precedents 3A and 3B).

5 Continuing residence for the survivor

Where two people (not husband and wife) live together they may feel that whilst they would like their entitlements in the jointly owned property to pass to their own families eventually, they would wish their companion to have the right to remain in the property for so long as he or she wishes. Precedent 10 is designed to cover such a situation and to allow a change of residence should this be required.

It is envisaged that the original tenants in common will be the trustees. On the death of one of them his personal representatives have the power of appointing a replacement trustee.

It will be observed (see p 26) that sale is to take place on the happening of a specified event, and that one of these is cohabitation of the survivor with another. Cohabitation is a difficult factual situation to define; this event is included so as to put the draftsman on notice that he should discuss the position with his clients.

The precedent can be adapted to a situation where there is a mortgage or no mortgage. The question of life policies would have to be considered separately.

6 Steps to be taken

(a) Stamp Duty

The declaration of trust is stampable 50p. Where the declaration in effect takes the form of an assignment (see Precedent 8) *ad valorem* stamp duty will be payable or certificate of value required.

(b) Copies

It is obviously prudent that each tenant in common has a copy of the declaration of trust to prove his entitlement.

PRECEDENTS

Precedent 1—property purchased by two persons as tenants in common. Straightforward agreement on division of sale proceeds in percentage shares. No mortgage.

THIS DECLARATION OF TRUST is made this   day of   19
BETWEEN   (1)   [X]   of   [address]   and   (2)   [Y]   of
[address]

WHEREAS:

(A) By a Conveyance/Transfer dated   the property ('the Property') details of which are contained in the Schedule hereto was conveyed/transferred to [X] and [Y] to be held by them [*unregistered land*] as tenants in common
or [*registered land*] subject to the usual joint proprietorship restriction

(B) The parties make this Declaration to set out their respective interests in the Property and its proceeds of sale and net rents and profits thereof until sale

NOW THIS DEED WITNESSES as follows:

1 THE parties hereto DECLARE that they hold the Property UPON TRUST to sell the same with power to postpone the sale and to hold the proceeds of sale (after deducting therefrom the costs of sale) and the net rents and profits until sale:
    (a)   as to [60%] for X absolutely
    (b)   as to [40%] for Y absolutely
  IN WITNESS whereof this declaration has been duly executed the day and year before written

SCHEDULE

[*unregistered land—brief description*]

[*registered land—Title No
      —Address*]

SIGNED AND DELIVERED as a
Deed by [X] in the
presence of:

SIGNED AND DELIVERED as a
Deed by [Y] in the
presence of:

Precedent 2—property purchased by two persons as tenants in common: details of purchase price and costs set out: division by reference to those. No mortgage.

THIS DECLARATION OF TRUST [*continue as Precedent 1*]

WHEREAS

(A) [As Precedent 1]

(B) [As Precedent [1] [continue] by reference to its purchase price and the costs of purchase thereof

NOW IT IS HEREBY DECLARED as follows:

1. The purchase price of the Property and the costs of purchase were as follows:

    Purchase price
    Stamp Duty
    Surveyors Costs
    H.M. Land Registry fees
    Other costs fees and disbursements

                                      Total £

2 It is agreed that X contributed £   to the total set out in Clause 1 hereof and Y contributed the balance of £

3 The parties hereto DECLARE that they hold the Property upon trust to sell the same with power to postpone the sale and to hold the proceeds of sale (after deducting therefrom the costs of sale) and the net rents and profits until sale:

(a)   as to [X's contribution] × net proceeds of sale
                  [Total]   for X absolutely

(b)   as to [Y's contribution] × net proceeds of sale
                  [Total]   for Y absolutely

    IN WITNESS etc

SCHEDULE

[*see Precedent 1*]

Attestation—[*as Precedent 1*]

Precedent 3A—deed of appointment of new trustees following death of one tenant in common. Unregistered land.

THIS DEED OF APPOINTMENT is made the   day of   19
BETWEEN (1) [Y] of   [address] ('the Appointor') and (2)
[A] of   [address] and [B]   [address] ('the
New Trustees')

WHEREAS:

(A) By a Conveyance ('the Conveyance') dated   and
made between (1) [vendors to X and Y] (2) [X] and the Appointor the
freehold property details of which are contained in the schedule was
conveyed to [X] and the Appointor in fee simple upon trust to sell the
same and to hold the net income until sale and the net proceeds of
sale in trust for themselves as tenants in common

(B) [X] died on [date]

(C) The Appointor wishes to appoint the New Trustees to be trustees
of the trusts of the Conveyance in place of [X]

NOW THIS DEED WITNESSES that in exercise of the statutory power
and of every other power here enabling the Appointor HEREBY
APPOINTS the New Trustees to be trustees of the trusts of the
Conveyance jointly with the Appointor and in place of [X]

    IN WITNESS whereof this deed has been duly executed the day
and year before written

SCHEDULE

[description of Property]

Attestation—[as Precedent 1]

Precedent 3B—registered land—transfer on appointment of new trustees

HM LAND REGISTRY

Land Registration Acts 1925 to 1986

County and district
(or London Borough)

Title No

Property

Date

1 For the purpose of effecting an appointment of new trustees I [Y] of
                transfer to myself the said [Y] and [A] of [address] and
[B] of [address] the land comprised in the title above mentioned [X]
having died on [insert date of death]

2 [XY] and [Z] as personal representatives of [X] signify their consent
to this transfer by signing the same. (see above p10)

3 It is certified that this instrument falls within Category A in the
Schedule to The Stamp Duty (Exempt Instruments) Regulations 1987

Attestation—[as Precedent 1]

Precedent 4—property purchased by two persons as tenants in common. Mortgage. Division in percentage shares.

THIS DECLARATION OF TRUST is made this   day of   19
BETWEEN   (1)   [X]   of   [address]   and   (2)   [Y]   of
[address]

WHEREAS:

(A) By a Conveyance/Transfer dated   the property ('the Property') details of which are contained in the Schedule hereto was conveyed/transferred to [X] and [Y] to be held by them [unregistered land] as tenants in common

or [registered land] subject to the usual joint proprietorship restriction

(B) By a Mortgage ('the Mortgage') dated   made between (1) the Parties hereto and (2) the [Building Society] the Property was charged to the [Building Society] to secure the sum of £

(C) The purchase price of the Property and the costs of purchase was £   provided as to £   by [X] and £   by [Y] and £   by the Mortgage.

(D) The parties make this Declaration to set out their respective interests in the Property and its proceeds of sale and net rents and profits thereof until sale

NOW THIS DEED WITNESSES as follows:

1 The parties hereto DECLARE that they hold the Property UPON TRUST to sell the same with power to postpone the sale and to hold the proceeds of sale (after deducting therefrom the costs of sale) and the net rents and profits until sale UPON TRUST:
(a)   to discharge the Morgage
(b)   as to the balance to divide the same:
  —   as to [%] for X absolutely
  —   as to [%] for Y absolutely

2 In this deed the expression 'the Mortgage' shall include any future substitution for the Mortgage or addition thereto

    IN WITNESS whereof this declaration has been duly executed the day and year before written

SCHEDULE

[unregistered land—brief description]
[registered land—Title No
            —Address]

Attestation—[as Precedent 1]

Precedent 5—property held by two persons as tenants in common subject to first mortgage. One joint owner wishing to raise additional money by way of second mortgage and indemnifying the other. Assumes plenty of equity in the property.

THIS DECLARATION OF TRUST is made this   day of   19
BETWEEN   (1)   [X]   of   [address]   and   (2)   [Y]   of [address]

WHEREAS:

(A) By a Conveyance/Transfer dated   the property ('the Property') details of which are contained in the Schedule hereto was conveyed/transferred to [X] and [Y] to be held by them

[unregistered land] as tenants in common

or [registered land] subject to the usual joint proprietorship restriction

(B) By a Mortgage ('the Mortgage') dated   19   and made between (1) the Parties hereto and (2) the [Building Society] the Property was charged to the [Building Society] to secure the sum of £

(C) X is indebted to [Bank] and Y has agreed to execute a second mortgage with X in favour of [Bank] provided that she is indemnified as herein set out

(D) The parties make this Declaration to set out their respective interests in the Property and its proceeds of sale and net rents and profits thereof until sale

NOW THIS DEED WITNESSES as follows:

1 X and Y DECLARE that they hold the Property henceforth UPON TRUST to sell the same with power to postpone the sale and to hold the proceeds of sale (after deducting therefrom the costs of sale) and the net rents and profits until sale:
    (a)   to discharge the Mortgage
    (b)   to discharge the Mortgage in favour of [Bank]
    (c)   to pay Y a sum equal to discharge the mortgage in favour of [Bank]
    (d)   to hold the balance:
        —   as to [%] for X
        —   as to [%] for Y

2 X covenants with Y to pay all payments required in connection with the mortgage in favour of [Bank] and to indemnify Y and keep her indemnified accordingly

  IN WITNESS etc

SCHEDULE

[see precedent 1]

Attestation—*[as precedent 1]*

Precedent 6—property held by trustees (X and Y) upon trust for X, Y and Z in unequal shares. No mortgage.

THIS DECLARATION OF TRUST is made this   day of   19
BETWEEN   (1)   [X]   of   [address]   and   [Y]   of
[address] ('the Trustees') which expression shall mean the trustee or
trustees   for   the   time   being   hereof)   and   (2)   [Z]   of
[address]

WHEREAS:

(A) By A Conveyance/Transfer dated   the property ('the
Property') details of which are contained in the Schedule hereto was
conveyed/transferred to the Trustees to be held by them

[unregistered land] upon the terms of this Declaration of Trust

or [registered land] subject to the usual joint proprietorship restriction

(B) The Trustees make this Declaration to set out the respective interests of [X] [Y] and [Z] in the Property and its proceeds of sale and net
rents and profits thereof until sale and [Z] has joined in the Declaration
to confirm his interest

NOW THIS DEED WITNESSES as follows:

1 The Trustees DECLARE that they hold the Property UPON TRUST
to sell the same with power to postpone the sale and to hold the proceeds of sale (after deducting therefrom the costs of sale) and the net
rents and profits until sale:
(a)   as to [40%] for X absolutely
(b)   as to [40%] for Y absolutely
(c)   as to [20%] for Z absolutely

2 [unregistered land only] The power of appointing new or additional
trustees of this Declaration and of the Conveyance shall be vested in
X, Y and Z or their respective personal representatives

   IN WITNESS etc

SCHEDULE

[description of property—Precedent 1]

Attestation—[as Precedent 1]

Precedent 7—property held by four trustees for themselves equally but charged to secure the borrowings of three of them.

THIS DECLARATION OF TRUST is made this   day of   19
BETWEEN (1) [A] of   [address] ('A') (2) [B] of [address] ('B') (3) [C] of   [address] ('C') and (4) [D] of [address] ('D')

WHEREAS:

(A) The parties are seised of the property ('the Property') details of which are contained in the Schedule hereto

(B) The Property is charged to [Bank] by way of three Legal Charges to secure sums advanced respectively to [A] [B] and [D] who have differing obligations to the [Bank]

(C) The parties make this Declaration to set out their respective interests in the Property and to give the indemnities herein contained

NOW THIS DEED WITNESSES as follows:

1 The parties hereto DECLARE that they hold the Property UPON TRUST to sell the same with power to postpone the sale and to hold the proceeds of sale (after deducting therefrom the costs of sale) and the net rents and profits until sale UPON TRUST:
(a) as to 25% thereof for [A]
(b) as to 25% thereof for [B]
(c) as to 25% thereof for [C]
(d) as to 25% thereof for [D]

2 Although as between the parties hereto and [Bank] each of the parties is liable to the [Bank] in respect of any obligations under the said Legal Charges IT IS HEREBY AGREED and each party hereto COVENANTS with each of the other parties to pay and discharge his or her respective obligations to the [Bank] and to keep the other parties and each of them and their respective estates indemnified in respect of any liability they or any of them might suffer by failure on his or her part to discharge such obligations and each party hereto hereby CHARGES his or her interest in the Property to the others to secure any monies which become due under this indemnity

IN WITNESS etc

SCHEDULE

[description of property—Precedent 1]

Attestation—[as Precedent 1]

Precedent 8—property held by four persons as tenants in common in equal shares. Now held for five persons equally by reason of sale.

THIS DECLARATION OF TRUST is made this   day of   19
BETWEEN (1) [A] of   [address] [B] of   [address]
[C] of   [address] and [D] of   [address] ('the
Trustees') and (2) [E] of   [address] ('the New Partner')

WHEREAS:

(A) By a Conveyance/Transfer dated   the property ('the
Property') details of which are contained in the schedule hereto was
conveyed/transferred to the Trustees to be held by them
[unregistered land] as tenants in common in equal shares
or [registered land] subject to the usual joint proprietorship restriction
and declared by them in a Declaration of Trust dated   to
be held for them as tenants in common in equal shares
(B) The New Partner having agreed to pay the sum of £   to the
Trustees to be received by them in equal shares it is agreed that on
receipt the Property will thenceforth be held by the Trustees as to one
fifth for each of themselves and the New Partner

NOW THIS DEED WITNESSES as follows:

1 In consideration of the sum of £   paid to the Trustees in equal
shares (receipt of which the Trustees hereby acknowledge) the
Trustees DECLARE that henceforth they will hold the Property and the
net proceeds of sale and the net rents and profits thereof until sale
UPON TRUST as to one fifth for each of themselves and the New
Partner and that the trusts of the Conveyance/Declaration of Trust
before referred to shall be varied accordingly

2 The New Partner covenants with the Trustees that henceforth he will
pay one fifth of the outgoings of the Property and will indemnify the
Trustees in respect of his one fifth share thereof

[3 It is hereby certified that the transaction hereby effected does not
form part of a larger transaction or of a series of transactions in respect
of which the amount or value or the aggregate amount or value of the
consideration exceeds £60,000.]

   IN WITNESS etc

SCHEDULE

[description of Property—Precedent 1]

Attestation—[as Precedent 1]

Precedent 9—property purchased by daughter (X) son-in-law (Y) and mother-in-law (A), X and Y holding legal title as joint tenants and mortgaging property, indemnity to mother-in-law.

THIS DECLARATION OF TRUST is made this   day of   19
BETWEEN (1) [X] and [Y] both of   ('the Trustees') and (2)
[A] of   ('Mrs A')

WHEREAS:

(A) By a Conveyance/Transfer dated   the property ('the Property') details of which are contained in the Schedule hereto was conveyed/transferred to the Trustees in fee simple in consideration of the sum of [£90,000]

(B) By a mortgage ('the Mortgage') dated   made between (1) the Trustees and (2) [Building Society] the Property was charged to the [Building Society] to secure the sum of £

(C) The total cost of the Property (including costs) was [£92,000] and was provided as follows:

The Trustees (including the sum borrowed under the Mortgage)	[62,000]
[Mrs A]	[30,000]
	[£92,000]

(D) The Trustees and Mrs A agree that the Trustees hold the Property upon the trusts herein set out

NOW THIS DEED WITNESSES as follows:

1 The Trustees hereby agree that they will not exercise their statutory power of sale of the Property without the written consent of [Mrs. A] during her lifetime [so long as it remains her principal residence]

2 Subject thereto the Trustees shall hold the Property and the proceeds of sale (after deducting therefrom the costs of sale) and the net rents and profits until sale UPON TRUST:

as to [62,000] × net proceeds of sale
        [92,000]   for the Trustees ('the Trustees' Share')
as to [30,000] × net proceeds of sale
        [92,000]   for [Mrs A]

3 As between themselves the Trustees shall hold the Trustees' Share in the Property as beneficial joint tenants

4(a) The Trustees hereby covenant with [Mrs A] (and for the benefit of her personal representatives) that they will pay all payments required under the Mortgage and that they will indemnify and keep indemnified [Mrs A] and her personal representatives against all costs liabilities and claims in respect of the Mortgage

(b) The Trustees further covenant with [Mrs A] and her personal representatives that on any sale of the Property they will discharge all monies owing under the Mortgage and all costs liabilities and claims in respect thereof out of the Trustees' Share

5 The power of appointing new or additional Trustees of this deed is vested in the Trustees and [Mrs A] jointly or the survivor or survivors of them

6 Every reference in this Deed to 'the Trustees' shall mean and include the trustee or trustees for the time being hereof

IN WITNESS etc

SCHEDULE

[description of Property—Precedent 1]

Attestation—*[as Precedent 1]*

Precedent 10—property held by two persons as tenants in common, contribution to purchase price specified. Right of survivor to continue to reside and change dwelling. Can be applied to mortgage or non-mortgage situation.

THIS DECLARATION OF TRUST is made the   day of   19
BY (1) [X] of   ('X') and [Y] of ('Y') (together called 'the Trustees' which expression shall include all other the trustee or trustees for the time being hereof)

WHEREAS:

(A) By a Conveyance/Transfer dated   the property briefly described in the Schedule hereto ('the Property') was conveyed/transferred to the Trustees to be held by them [*unregistered land*] as tenants in common or [*registered land*] subject to the usual joint proprietorship restriction

[(B) By a mortgage ('the Mortgage') dated   and made between (1) the Trustees and (2) [*Building Society*] the Property was charged to [*Building Socicty*] to secure the sum of £   ]

(C) or (B) The Trustees make this Declaration to set out their respective interests in the Property by reference to its purchase price and the costs of purchase thereof and the trusts powers and provisions subject to which the Property is held

NOW IT IS HEREBY DECLARED as follows:

1 The following expressions shall have the following meanings:

(a) 'the dwelling' shall mean ALL THAT the Property and any house bungalow flat or maisonette purchased by the Trustees in accordance with the provisions hereof in substitution for the Property

(b) 'the residing party' shall mean such of X or Y as shall reside or continue to reside in the dwelling after the death of the first to die of X or Y

(c) 'the specified events' shall mean:
    (i)   the death of the survivor of X and Y
    (ii) the marriage or re-marriage of either X or Y after the death of the first to die of X or Y
    [(iii) the co-habitation of the survivor with any other person]
whichever shall first occur

(d) 'the net proceeds of sale' shall mean the proceeds of sale of the dwelling after payment of the costs of sale [and repayment of the Mortgage]
2 The purchase price of the Property and the costs of purchase were as follows:

Purchase Price
Inland Revenue Stamp Duty
Surveyors fees
H.M. Land Registry fees
Legal fees
Other costs fees and disbursements

Total £

3 It is agreed that X contributed £   to the Total set out in Clause 2 hereof and Y contributed £   [and the balance was provided by the Mortgage]

4 The Trustees shall hold the dwelling UPON TRUST to sell the same but with the full power to postpone such sale

5(a) Without prejudice to the immediate binding trust for sale imposed by the preceding clause the Trustees may permit the residing party to reside in and continue to reside in the dwelling without payment therefor made by the residing party to the Trustees and provided none of the specified events shall happen the Trustees shall permit the residing party to continue to reside in the dwelling until such time as the residing party shall have signified to the Trustees in writing the wish no longer so to reside

(b) The residing party covenants with the Trustees and the personal representatives of the first of X or Y to die that he will pay all payments required under the Mortgage and that he will indemnify and keep indemnified the Trustees and the personal representatives aforesaid against all cost liabilities and claims in respect of the Mortgage

6(a) As often as the residing party shall so request in writing the Trustees may at their discretion sell the dwelling currently held by them upon the trusts of the preceding clauses and with the net proceeds of sale purchase any dwelling designated by the residing party (but if such dwelling be leasehold only if the residue of the term of years granted by the lease exceeds 60 years at the date of such designation) the total cost of which (including all legal and surveyors fees other costs fees and disbursements and stamp duty and HM Land Registry fees if appropriate) does not exceed those proceeds

(b) The Trustees shall be entitled to purchase any dwelling as aforesaid at a price in excess of such proceeds if such excess shall be provided by the residing party in which case such proportion of the future sale proceeds as such excess shall bear to the cost of purchase shall belong to the residing party absolutely on any such future sale but in the event that the future sale proceeds of the dwelling shall be less than the cost of purchase then the excess shall be reduced pro rata to the total reduction in value of the dwelling as compared with the cost of purchase

(c) If at the time of the purchase of any dwelling there should remain any surplus money in the hands of the Trustees they shall hold such surplus money upon the trusts of Clause 8 hereof

7 The residing party hereby covenants with the Trustees that for as long as he shall continue to reside in the dwelling he will pay the rent (if any) and other outgoings and keep the dwelling in good repair and insured comprehensively to its full value in an insurance office approved by the Trustees and in the joint names of the residing party and the Trustees and he shall within seven days of any demand being made produce to the Trustees or one of them such policy of insurance and the last receipt for premium in respect thereof and will comply with all the terms and conditions affecting the dwelling as if the residing party was the absolute owner thereof and was bound thereby and the residing party further covenants to indemnify the Trustees and each of them and their respective estates and effects against any loss damage liability charge or expense caused by or arising out of the failure by him to observe any of the terms and conditions aforesaid

8 Upon the happening of any one of the specified events the Trustees shall carry out the said trust for sale and shall stand possessed of the net proceeds of sale subject to the provisions of Clause 6

(a)   as to [X's contribution] × net proceeds of sale
              [Total]   for X absolutely or his
                                personal representatives
(b)   as to [Y's contribution] × net proceeds of sale
              [Total]   for Y absolutely or his
                                personal representatives

and until such sale shall take place the residing party if remaining in occupation shall remain liable to pay the outgoings referred to in clause 7 hereof and keep the dwelling in good repair and insured as aforesaid

9 The Trustees and each of them shall be entitled to be indemnified out of the proceeds of sale of the dwelling against all costs expenses damages claims and demands incurred or sustained by them by reason of their holding the dwelling upon the trusts hereof and in fur-therance of such indemnity the Trustees shall be deemed to have all the powers (including the power of sale) given to a mortgagee under the Law of Property Act 1925 and shall be entitled to exercise the same to indemnify themselves or either of them under the provisions of this clause

10(a) If after written demand made by the Trustees in that behalf the residing party shall have failed within a period of six weeks from the date thereof to put the dwelling in good repair or to insure the same as aforesaid the Trustees may in their entire discretion effect or cause to be effected such repairs as are necessary to put the dwelling into good repair or effect such policy of insurance and the Trustees and each of them shall be entitled to an indemnity in respect of any costs or charges incurred by them in so doing and in furtherance of such indemnity the Trustees shall be deemed to have the like powers to those set out in the preceding clause hereof PROVIDED ALWAYS that the Trustees shall not be liable to see to any such insurance or repair and shall be under no liability in respect thereof

(b) The Trustees may borrow money using the dwelling as security if required on such terms as to interest and repayment and otherwise as they may think fit for the purpose of carrying out such repairs as aforesaid

11 The power of appointing a trustee in substitution for [X] shall be vested in [X] during his lifetime and after his death in his personal representatives and the power of appointing a trustee in substitution for [Y] shall be vested in [Y] during her lifetime and after her death in her personal representatives

[12 Charging clause if professional trustees:

Any trustee hereof engaged in a profession or business shall be entitled to be paid all usual professional or other charges for business transacted and acts done by him or by a partner of his in connection with the trusts hereof (whether or not in the course of his profession or business) including acts which a trustee not being in a profession or business could have done personally]

IN WITNESS etc

SCHEDULE

[description of Property—see Precedent 1]

Attestation—*[as Precedent 1]*

3

Property purchased by beneficial joint tenants Subsequent adjustment of interests

1   Introduction

In the majority of cases, property purchased by a husband and wife is purchased by them as beneficial joint tenants so that in the event of the death of one of them, the whole property passes to the survivor by operation of law. Such a situation is not of course merely limited to husband and wife.

Following a change in circumstances, or a reappraisal of circumstances it may be considered appropriate to sever the joint tenancy so that the parties' interests are defined. Chapter 2 mentioned reasons why a property might be held as tenants in common.

Alternatively there are circumstances where it is appropriate that property held by tenants in common should subsequently be held by them as beneficial joint tenants (see Precedent 14), for instance, where cohabitees, instead of preserving their separate interests, wish to ensure that the property passes to the survivor of them on death outside the terms of any will or operation of the rules of intestacy.

2   Severance

The procedure for severance differs depending upon whether title to the property is registered or not.

(a)   Unregistered land

Section 36(2) of the Law of Property Act 1925 provides for severance of a joint tenancy either by:
(1) a notice in writing given by one joint tenant to the other; or
(2) the doing of such other acts or things as would, in the case of
    personal estate, have been effectual to sever the tenancy in equity.
The mere issue of matrimonial proceedings for a property adjustment order does not automatically sever a joint tenancy (*Harris v
Goddard* [1983] 1 WLR 203) but the issue of proceedings under s 17
of the Married Women's Property Act 1882 can cause severance to
occur (*Re Draper's Conveyance* [1969] 3 Ch 486) as does the bankruptcy of one of the parties (*Re Gorman (a bankrupt)* [1990] 1 WLR
616), severance taking place at the date of the act of bankruptcy, not
at the date of adjudication (*Re Dennis* (1995) *The Independent*,
22 May).
    The joint tenants may agree that the joint tenancy should be
severed, but if so they should properly evidence that fact. In *Nielson-
Jones v Fedden* [1975] Ch 222 it was held that it was not sufficient for
the husband and wife to sign a memorandum to the effect that the
husband was to have a free hand to sell the property and use the
money to buy a new house for himself although in *Burgess v
Rawnsley* [1975] Ch 429 it was held that a beneficial joint tenancy
was severed by the oral agreement of one joint tenant to sell her
share in the property to the other, even though that agreement was
not specifically enforceable. Similarly, drafting an agreement in the
course of matrimonial negotiations can be indicative of an agreement to sever even if the agreement is not executed (*Hunter v
Babbage* [1994] EGCS 8) although the actual facts would be looked
at very carefully.
    Service of a notice of severance (see Precedent 11A) would appear
to be effective to sever the joint tenancy if properly addressed to the
other joint tenant and received at the property concerned.
    It would appear not to matter that the party to whom the notice
is addressed does not acknowledge receipt nor even if the party
addressed never actually receives the notice itself (see *Re 88 Berkeley
Road, London NW9; Rickwood v Turnsek* [1971] Ch 648, and generally as to methods of severance, (1976) *Conveyancer NS*, col 40,
p 77).
    Whilst the notice itself may be sufficient to sever the beneficial

joint tenancy, to prevent a conveyance by the survivor, either through ignorance or fraud, it is prudent to endorse a memorandum on the last conveyance to the effect that severance has taken place. This should be sufficient to put a purchaser on notice so that he insists on paying the purchase monies to two trustees or a trust corporation so as to obtain a good receipt (Law of Property Act 1925, s 27).

Under the Law of Property (Joint Tenants) Act 1964 a conveyance by the survivor of joint tenants as 'beneficial owner' was sufficient to entitle any purchaser to presume that the survivor was no longer a trustee. The Law of Property Act (Miscellaneous Provisions) Act 1994 which came into force on 1 July 1995 requires any conveyance/transfer to contain a statement that such survivor is solely and beneficially interested in the property.

In the absence therefore of any memorandum on the last conveyance, or the registration of a petition or receiving order in bankruptcy at HM Land Charges Registry coupled with the statement above, a purchaser from a surviving joint tenant would get good title.

(b)   Registered land

Section 74 of the Land Registration Act 1925 provides that, as far as possible, reference to trusts shall be excluded from the register. A notice of severance or declaration of trust whilst being effective in equity, would have no effect on the register unless it was completed by an application to register a restriction so that the register shows that the survivor of the former two joint tenants is no longer able to give a valid receipt for capital monies (see Precedent 11C).

Severance and the above application result in the obligatory entry of a Form 62 restriction on the register under the Land Registration Act 1925, s 63:

'No disposition by a sole proprietor of the land (not being a Trust Corporation) under which capital money arises is to be registered except under an order of the registrar or of the Court.'

It will be appreciated that the registration of a restriction does not specify the shares in which the net proceeds of sale of the prop-

erty are to be held so there should be a declaration of trust speci-
fying those shares. Registration of a restriction does at least
provide some protection and room for manoeuvre in the event of
the death of a former joint tenant whilst such a declaration is being
finalised.

3   The shares of the former joint tenants following severance

These shares can be agreed and specified in a declaration of trust,
and this is obviously the sensible course. In the absence of agreement
it was previously thought that severance where no shares are agreed
operated to create a tenancy in common in equal shares (see
Megarry and Wade, *Real Property* (5th edn, Stevens, 1984), p 430
and *R v Porter* [1990] 1 WLR 1260 where the Court of Appeal held
that in a joint venture, in the absence of any evidence, the court was
entitled to assume equal sharing).

In *Goodman v Gallant* [1986] 1 All ER 311, the conveyance was
to the parties as beneficial joint tenants, Mrs Goodman subsequently severing the joint tenancy by notice in writing, stating
that 'the said property shall henceforth belong to you and me in
equal shares', but later seeking a declaration that she should be
entitled to three-quarters of the proceeds of sale. The Court of
Appeal held that in the absence of any claim for rectification or
rescission of the original conveyance, evidence could not be
subsequently given in support of an unequal division following
severance.

In *Springette v Defoe* [1992] Fam Law 459 the court decided that
where there had been no discussion between the parties about their
respective beneficial interests, the court could not infer an intention
of equal shares; the shares were presumed to be in proportion to
their respective contributions.

With the exception of contested matrimonial cases, where consideration of the presumption of advancement will be a factor, the
extent of each party's entitlement in the absence of agreement would
appear logically to be by reference to their respective contributions,
although ultimately any disagreement would fall to be determined
by the courts.

4   Contents of the declaration

These have been mentioned in Chapter 2 (see pp 10–11). Where there is a 'friendly' severance, the parties may decide merely to evidence that fact and set out the agreed shares (see Precedent 12), but the declaration can be extended to cover responsibility for the mortgage (see Precedent 13) and obligations as to insurance and repair (see Precedents 15 and 17).

5   Restrictions on the appointment of new trustees

Following severance, on the death of a trustee if there is to be a sale a new trustee will need to be appointed of the conveyance (in unregistered land) so that a purchaser receives a good receipt for capital monies (LPA 1925, s 27) or for the purposes of complying with the terms of the normal joint proprietorship restriction in the case of registered land (see above, p 32).

In general, where there is a non-confrontational severance of a joint tenancy, the parties will probably be content that the survivor of them has power to appoint a new trustee under the provisions of the Trustee Act 1925, s 36 (see Precedents 3A and 3B).

However, this may not be considered satisfactory where there has for instance been a matrimonial dispute or where there is distrust such as in the case of a second marriage.

Whilst limitations on the appointment can be contained in the declaration of trust, it is only in registered land that these are actually brought onto the legal title by way of a restriction to that effect. The following may be considered:

    (a) a replacement trustee on the death of X to be appointed by his personal representatives. This inevitably involves some little delay whilst a grant of representation to X's estate is obtained; *or*

    (b) the appointment of a replacement trustee on the death of X to require the consent of X's personal representatives.

6   Steps to be taken

(a)   Stamp Duty

The declaration of trust is stampable 50p.

(b) Copies

It is prudent that each tenant in common has a copy of the declaration of trust to prove his entitlement.

(c) HM Land Registry

Application to register a restriction being required (see above) no fee is now payable.

(d) Will

Where severance takes place it is appropriate that the former joint tenants review their respective wills to deal now with their separate interest in the property.

PRECEDENTS

Precedent 11A—Notice of Severance by one joint tenant to the other severing joint tenancy. Unregistered land.

To [*full name and address of other joint tenant*]

I HEREBY GIVE YOU NOTICE severing our joint tenancy in equity of and in the Property details of which are given in the Schedule hereto now held by yourself and myself as joint tenants both at law and in equity and henceforth the Property shall be held by us as tenants in common in:
— equal shares (or whatever shares are agreed)
— or upon the terms of a Declaration of Trust signed by us

I REQUEST that you acknowledge receipt of this notice by signing and returning the Duplicate Notice enclosed.

SCHEDULE

[*description of Property*]

Date
Signed (signature of joint tenant giving notice]

Duplicate
I acknowledge receipt of this Notice of Severance of which the above is a duplicate
Date
Signed [signature of recipient]

Precedent 11B—Unregistered land. Memorandum of severance to be endorsed on last Conveyance.

MEMORANDUM

By a Notice of Severance dated   addressed by the within named [X] to the within named [Y] the beneficial joint tenancy herein created was severed.

Precedent 11C—Registered Land. Application to enter a restriction (Form 75).

HM LAND REGISTRY

Land Registration Acts 1925 to 1986

County and district
or London Borough
Title Number
Property
Date
We [X] of   and [Y] of   apply to the Registrar
to enter the following restriction against the title above referred to:

Restriction: No disposition by one proprietor of the land (being the survivor of joint proprietors and not being a trust corporation) under which capital money arises is to be registered except under an Order of the Registrar or of the Court.

SIGNED etc [*both parties*]

Precedent 12—property held by beneficial joint tenants, severance, property henceforth to be held in defined shares. No mortgage.

THIS DECLARATION OF TRUST is made this   day of   19

BETWEEN   (1)   [X]   of   [address]   and   (2)   [Y]   of
[address]

WHEREAS:

(A) By a Conveyance/Transfer dated   the property ('the Property') details of which are contained in the Schedule hereto was conveyed/transferred to [X] and [Y] to be held by them
[*unregistered land*] as beneficial joint tenants
or [*registered land*] on the basis that the survivor of them could give a good receipt for capital monies being beneficial joint tenants.

(B) The parties have agreed that their joint tenancy of the Property should be severed and that henceforth their interests in the Property and its proceeds of sale and net rents and profits thereof until sale shall be held as hereinafter mentioned.

NOW THIS DEED WITNESSES as follows:
1 The parties hereto DECLARE that with effect from the date hereof they HOLD the Property in fee simple UPON TRUST to sell the same and to hold the proceeds of sale (after deducting therefrom the costs of sale) and the net rents and profits until sale as to [60%] for [X] and as to [40%] for [Y] as tenants in common
2 [*registered land*] The parties hereto covenant with each other to sign such application as may be necessary to enter the appropriate restriction at HM Land Registry to give effect to this Deed
     IN WITNESS etc

SCHEDULE

[description of Property—see Precedent 1]

Attestation—*[as Precedent 1]*

Note:
  (a)   unregistered title—put Memorandum on last Conveyance (see Precedent 11B)
  (b)   registered title—apply to HMLR on Form 75 (see Precedent 11C)

Precedent 13—property held by beneficial joint tenants subject to mortgage. Severance and agreement to hold and pay mortgage in defined shares.

THIS DECLARATION OF TRUST is made this   day of   19
BETWEEN   (1)   [X]   of   [address]   and   (2)   [Y]   of
            [address]

WHEREAS:

(A) [As Precedent 12 recital (A)]

(B) By a Mortgage ('the Mortgage') dated   and made
between (1) the parties hereto and (2) [Building Society] the Property
was charged to the said Society to secure the sum of £

(C) The parties have agreed that their joint tenancy should be severed
and that henceforth their interests in the Property and its proceeds of
sale and net rents and profits thereof until sale shall be held as hereinafter mentioned subject to the Mortgage

NOW THIS DEED WITNESSES as follows:

1 The parties hereto DECLARE that with effect from the date hereof
they HOLD the Property in fee simple SUBJECT to the Mortgage
UPON TRUST to sell the same and to hold the proceeds of sale (after
deducting therefrom the costs of sale) and the net rents and profits
until sale as to [60%] for [X] and as to [40%] for [Y] as tenants in
common AND upon the basis that the Mortgage shall be repaid as to
[60%] by [X] and as to [40%] by [Y]

2 The parties hereto covenant with each other to pay the payments
due under the Mortgage in the same percentage as their entitlement
as set out in Clause 1 and to indemnify the other and his estate and
effects against all costs claims and demands in respect of the
Mortgage to the limit of the percentage before mentioned

3 [registered land] [As Precedent 12 clause 2]

   IN WITNESS etc

SCHEDULE

[description of Property—see Precedent 1]

Attestation—[as Precedent 1]

Precedent 14A—property held as tenants in common in equal shares now to be held by them as beneficial joint tenants.

THIS DECLARATION OF TRUST is made this   day of   19
BETWEEN   (1)   [X]   of   [address]   and   (2)   [Y]   of
                 [address]

WHEREAS:

(A) The property ('the Property') details of which are contained in the Schedule hereto
[unegistered land] is presently held by the parties hereto as trustees for themselves as tenants in common in equal shares
or [registered land] is registered in the names of the parties hereto subject to the restriction that the survivor of them is unable to give a valid receipt for capital monies
(B) The parties have agreed that henceforth they should hold the Property as beneficial joint tenants

NOW THIS DEED WITNESSES as follows:

1 The parties hereto DECLARE that with effect from the date hereof they shall hold the Property UPON TRUST to sell the same and hold the net proceeds of sale and the net income until sale in trust for themselves as beneficial joint tenants

2 [registered land] The parties hereto covenant to apply to HM Land Registry to cancel the restriction recited above and to amend the register to the effect that the survivor of them can give a valid receipt for capital money arising on a disposition of the land comprised in the title below mentioned

   IN WITNESS etc

SCHEDULE

[description of Property—see Precedent 1]

Attestation—[as Precedent 1]

**Precedent 14B—registered land. Application to withdraw
Restriction to give effect to Precedent 14A.**

HM LAND REGISTRY

Land Registration Acts 1925 to 1986

County and district
or London Borough
Title Number
Property
Date

[X] of   [address] and [Y] of   [address]
hereby apply to the Registrar to withdraw the restriction registered on
[date as from Proprietorship Register] against the title above referred
to.

[X] and [Y] declare that the survivor of them can give a valid receipt for
capital money arising on a disposition of the land

Attestation—[as Precedent 1]

Precedent 15—matrimonial home originally held by husband and wife as beneficial joint tenants. Tenancy now severed and house to be held upon terms of Court Order. Unregistered and registered land. No mortgage.

Notice of Severance to be endorsed on last Conveyance (Precedent 11B) or application for restriction at HMLR (Precedent 11C)

THIS DECLARATION OF TRUST is made the   day of   19

BY   [*Husband*] of   ('the Husband') and [*Wife*] of   ('the Wife')

WHEREAS:

(A) By a conveyance ('the Conveyance') dated   and made between (1)   and (2)   the Husband and the Wife the Property briefly described in the Schedule hereto was conveyed to the Husband and the Wife in fee simple as beneficial joint tenants

(B) Following an Order of [Deputy] District Judge   in the County Court dated   in proceedings between the parties hereto bearing number   the joint tenancy created by the Conveyance was severed as the parties hereto hereby admit and it was ordered that the Property be held upon the terms hereinafter mentoned

[or (A) The Husband and the Wife are registered as the proprietors at HM Land Registry of the property briefly described in the Schedule hereto on the basis that the survivor of them can give a good receipt for capital monies

(B) Following an Order of [Deputy] District Judge   in the County Court dated   and in proceedings between the Husband and the Wife bearing number   it was ordered that the Property be held upon the terms hereinafter mentioned]

NOW IT IS HEREBY DECLARED as follows:

1 In pursuance of the Court Order as from [*date of Court Order*] the parties shall HOLD the Property in fee simple UPON TRUST to sell the same and to stand possessed of the proceeds of sale (after deducting therefrom the costs of sale) and the net rents and profits until sale in trust for the parties hereto as to [60] per cent for the Husband and as to [40] per cent for the Wife and otherwise upon the terms of the said Court Order

2 The trustees hereof from time to time shall have power (until the expiration of 21 years from the death of the survivor of the Husband and the Wife) to sell mortgage charge lease or otherwise dispose of all or any part of the Property with all the powers in that behalf of an absolute owner

3 The Wife covenants with the Husband that she will keep the Property in good repair and insured comprehensively to its full value in an insurance office approved by the Husband and in the joint names of herself and the Husband and she shall within seven days of any demand being made produce to the Husband such policy of insurance and the last receipt for premium in respect thereof

IN WITNESS etc

SCHEDULE

[brief description of property from title documents]

Attestation—[as Precedent 1]

Precedent 16—matrimonial home originally held by husband and wife as beneficial joint tenants. Tenancy now severed and house held upon terms of Court Order. Mortgage—husband to be responsible until sale.

Notice of Severance to be endorsed on last Conveyance (Precedent 11B) or application for restriction at HM Land Registry (Precedent 11C)

THIS DECLARATION OF TRUST is made the   day of   19
BY [*Husband*] of   ('the Husband') and [*Wife*] of   ('the Wife')

WHEREAS:

(A) [*Recital of conveyance to Husband and Wife—Precedent 15 recital (A)*]

(B) By a Mortgage ('the Mortgage') dated   and made between (1) the Husband and the Wife and (2) the Building Society ('the Society') the Property was charged to the Society to secure the sum of £

(C) The sum of £   is now owing to the Society on the security of the Mortgage

(D) By an order of [Deputy] District Judge   in the County Court dated   in proceedings between the Husband and the Wife bearing number   the joint tenancy created by the Conveyance was severed as the Husband and the Wife hereby admit and it was ordered that the Property be held upon the terms hereinafter mentioned with the Husband being solely responsible for the monies due under the Mortgage

NOW IT IS HEREBY DECLARED:

1 Pursuant to the Order as from [*date of Court Order*] the Husband and the Wife shall hold the Property in fee simple UPON TRUST to sell the same and to stand possessed of the net proceeds of sale (which for the avoidance of doubt shall mean the sum remaining after discharge of the Mortgage and payment of all the costs of sale) and the net rents and profits until sale in trust for the parties as to   per cent for the Husband and as to   per cent for the Wife SUBJECT to the Mortgage and otherwise upon the terms of the Court Order

2 [*Powers of Trustees—see Precedent 15, clause 2—unless these are already contained in the original conveyance to the husband and wife)*]

3 The Husband covenants with the Wife that with effect from [*usually a date specified in the Court Order*] and until the Property be sold he will pay and discharge all principal monies interest costs and other monies secured by or henceforth to become payable under the

Mortgage and will at all times indemnify and keep indemnified the Wife and her estate and effects against all proceedings costs claims and demands in respect thereof

4 [covenant to repair—see Precedent 15, clause 3]

IN WITNESS etc

SCHEDULE

[*brief description of property from title documents*]

Attestation—[*as Precedent 1*]

Precedent 17—Dwellinghouse held by trustees upon trust until the happening of certain events and then for former husband and wife in unequal shares, occupying wife to be responsible for repairs etc. Power to change the property for another. Registered or unregistered land.

THIS DECLARATION OF TRUST is made the   day of   19
BY (1) [X] of   and [Y] of   (together called
'the Trustees' which expression shall include all other the trustee or
trustees for the time being hereof) and (2) [Wife] of   ('the
Wife')

WHEREAS:

(A) By a Conveyance/Transfer bearing the same date as but exe-
cuted before this Declaration and made between (1) [Husband] and
[Wife] and (2) the Trustees the property briefly described in the
Schedule hereto ('the Property') was conveyed/transferred to the
Trustees

(B) The Trustees make this Declaration to set out the trusts and the
powers and provisions subject to which the Property is held

NOW IT IS HEREBY DECLARED as follows:

1 The following expressions shall have the following meanings:
(a) 'the dwelling' shall mean ALL THAT the Property and any house
bungalow flat or maisonette purchased by the Trustees in accordance
with the provisions hereof in substitution for the Property
(b) 'the specified events' shall mean:
  (i)(a) the eighteenth birthday of [A—youngest child] who was born
          on   [date] or
    (b) the date upon which [A] shall cease full time education
          whichever is the later or
  (ii) the death of the Wife or
  (iii) the re-marriage of the Wife
whichever shall first occur
(c) 'the net proceeds of sale' shall mean the proceeds of sale of the
dwelling after payment of the costs of sale

2 The Trustees shall hold the dwelling UPON TRUST to sell the same
but with the full power to postpone such sale

3 Without prejudice to the immediate binding trust for sale imposed
by the preceding clause the Trustees may permit the Wife to reside in
and continue to reside in the dwelling without payment therefor made
by her to the Trustees and provided none of the specified events shall
happen the Trustees shall permit the Wife to continue to reside in the
dwelling until such time as she shall have signified to the Trustees in
writing her wish no longer so to reside

4(a) As often as the Wife shall so request in writing the Trustees may at their discretion sell the dwelling currently held by them upon the trusts of the preceding clauses and with the net proceeds of sale purchase any dwelling designated by the Wife (but if such dwelling be leasehold only if the residue of the term of years granted by the lease exceeds 60 years at the date of such designation) the total cost of which (including all legal and surveyors fees other costs fees and disbursements and stamp duty and HM Land Registry fees if appropriate) does not exceed those proceeds

(b) The Trustees shall be entitled to purchase any dwelling as aforesaid at a price in excess of such proceeds if such excess shall be provided by the Wife in which case such proportion of the future sale proceeds as such excess shall bear to the cost of purchase shall belong to the Wife absolutely on any such future sale but in the event that the future sale proceeds of the dwelling shall be less than the cost of purchase then the excess shall be reduced pro rata to the total reduction in value of the dwelling as compared with the cost of purchase

(c) If at the time of the purchase of any dwelling there should remain any surplus money in the hands of the Trustees they shall hold such surplus money upon the trusts of Clause 6 hereof

5 The Wife hereby covenants with the Trustees that for as long as she shall continue to reside in the dwelling she will pay the rent (if any) and other outgoings and keep the dwelling in good repair and insured comprehensively to its full value in an insurance office approved by the Trustees and in the joint names of herself and the Trustees and she shall within seven days of any demand being made produce to the Trustees or one of them such policy of insurance and the last receipt for premium in respect thereof and she will comply with all the terms and conditions affecting the dwelling as if she was the absolute owner thereof and was bound thereby and the Wife further covenants to indemnify the Trustees and each of them and their respective estates and effects against any loss damage liability charge or expense caused by or arising out of the failure by her to observe any of the terms and conditions aforesaid

6 Upon the happening of any one of the specified events the Trustees shall carry out the said trust for sale and shall stand possessed of the net proceeds of sale subject to the provisions of Clause 4:

   (i)   as to 60 per cent for [Husband] or his personal representatives (as the case may be)

   (ii) as to 40 per cent for the Wife or her personal representatives (as the case may be) less any monies due to the Trustees by reason of the indemnities herein contained

and until such sale shall take place the Wife if remaining in occupation shall remain liable to pay the outgoings referred to in clause 5 hereof and keep the dwelling in good repair and insured as aforesaid

7 The Trustees and each of them shall be entitled to be indemnified out of the proceeds of sale of the dwelling against all costs expenses damages claims and demands incurred or sustained by them by reason of their holding the dwelling upon the trusts hereof and in furtherance of such indemnity the Trustees shall be deemed to have all the powers (including the power of sale) given to a mortgagee under the Law of Property Act 1925 and shall be entitled to exercise the same to indemnify themselves or either of them under the provisions of this clause

8(a) If after written demand made by the Trustees in that behalf the Wife shall have failed within a period of six weeks from the date thereof to put the dwelling in good repair or to insure the same as aforesaid the Trustees may in their entire discretion effect or cause to be effected such repairs as are necessary to put the dwelling into good repair or effect such policy of insurance and the Trustees and each of them shall be entitled to an indemnity in respect of any costs or charges incurred by them in so doing and in furtherance of such indemnity the Trustees shall be deemed to have the like powers to those set out in the preceding clause hereof PROVIDED ALWAYS that the Trustees shall not be liable to see to any such insurance or repair and shall be under no liability in respect thereof
(b) The Trustees may borrow money using the dwelling as security if required on such terms as to interest and repayment and otherwise as they may think fit for the purpose of carrying out such repairs as aforesaid

9 The power of appointing a trustee in substitution for [X] shall be vested in [Husband] during his lifetime and after his death in his personal representatives and the power of appointing a trustee in substitution for [Y] shall be vested in the Wife during her lifetime and after her death in her personal representatives

[10 Charging clause if professional trustees:

Any trustee hereof engaged in a profession or business shall be entitled to be paid all usual professional or other charges for business transacted and acts done by him or by a partner of his in connection with the trusts hereof (whether or not in the course of his profession or business) including acts which a trustee not being in a profession or business could have done personally]
    IN WITNESS etc

SCHEDULE

[description of Property—see Precedent 1]

Attestation—[as Precedent 1]

4

Legal owner of dwellinghouse holding for another (or for self and another)

1   Introduction

It is not unusual for the sole owner of a dwellinghouse to want to recognise the equity that someone else may have contributed. Whilst this can be solved by the owner conveying/transferring the property into joint names to be held as a joint tenants or tenants in common (in which latter case a declaration of trust should be made; see Precedent 1), this may not be convenient (for examples see below) and a declaration of trust, whilst not psychologically the same, can achieve the same result in equity.

Similarly, an individual may have a personal right to buy a property but be financially unable to do so. Again, if the money is provided by someone else, the provider's interest can be recognised by the individual making a declaration of trust.

2   Nominee conveyance

If mere anonymity is required at the time of the purchase, then the appropriate course is for an individual to complete the purchase and then immediately make a 'nominee conveyance' to the true purchaser (see precedents in *Kelly's Draftsman* (16th edn, 1994, Butterworths), p 909 and *Encyclopaedia of Forms and Precedents* (5th edn, Butterworths), Vol 36, p 718).

Such a situation may arise where for instance an agent completes the purchase of a property bought at auction and immediately fol-

lowing completion transfers the property to the party for whom he
acted and who put up the purchase price.

If, however, it is intended that the property should remain in the
nominee's name for the time being, then the appropriate course is for
the nominee to make a declaration of trust (see Precedent 18). This
can leave the real owner a little exposed should the trustee be
unscrupulous, and the real owner should be advised:

(1) to ensure that he (the real owner) holds the title documents;
(2) in the case of unregistered land, to consider the appoint-
    ment of a further trustee (on the grounds that one person
    may be unscrupulous but two are less likely to be so!) and
    to register a caution against first registration, so that the
    real owner will learn about any application to HM Land
    Registry and have the opportunity to oppose it.

    The caution must be in statutory Form 13 (printed
    form), be signed by the cautioner or his solicitor, contain
    an address (or two) for service in the United Kingdom and
    sufficiently identify the land, preferably by plan. It must be
    accompanied by a statutory declaration showing the inter-
    est the cautioner claims in the land, in this case that he is
    the beneficial owner; and
(3) in the case of registered land, to enter a restriction to the
    effect that no disposition can take place without the
    consent of the real owner during his lifetime or his personal
    representatives after his death (see Precedent 24).

3   The council house

The Housing Act 1985 has given occupiers of houses owned by their
local authority or New Town Development Corporation a right to
buy the house and discounts on the value of the property depending
upon the length of occupation can make such a purchase an attrac-
tive proposition.

The discount is only available to the occupying tenant, who is
often elderly or without means to purchase. However, someone
within the family may be prepared to provide the finances necessary
for the purchase and it is this contributor's position that should be
protected.

This can be done by:

(1) a declaration of trust being made by the legal owner (the council tenant); and

(2) registering a restriction at HM Land Registry. The question of unregistered land does not arise because any such purchase is subject to compulsory registration of title (Housing Act 1985, s 154).

A relevant disposal (see Housing Act 1985, s 159) of the dwelling within three years of purchase (Housing and Planning Act 1986, s 2(3)) triggers repayment of the discount, the amount being by reference to the number of years since purchase. It is worth recalling that the vesting of the whole of the dwellinghouse in a person taking under a will or on intestacy, or if the disposal is pursuant to a property adjustment order in matrimonial proceedings where continuing occupation is envisaged, are exempt disposals and do not trigger repayment of the discount (Housing Act 1985, s 160).

It has been suggested to the author that the sale of a council house to the occupant who subsequently makes a declaration of trust that he holds the property for the provider of the purchaser price is itself a relevant disposal triggering repayment of the discount. Apart from the fact that the local authority has no way of finding out about the declaration (as it is off the title), no authority for this proposition has been found by the author.

It is important that the parties (ie the person with the right to buy ('the occupier') and the contributor) consider:

(1) is there to be a provision at the end of the repayment of discount period whereby the contributor can require the property to be transferred to his name? This will probably depend upon the agreed 'stake' (if any) of the occupier in the property;

(2) should the position of the occupier be protected by a lease so as to give security of tenure or a provision agreed so that the property cannot be sold without his consent? This is important—the elderly council tenant could count on security of tenure. If her son provides the purchase price and then has matrimonial proceedings, the estranged daughter-in-law might press for a sale of the former council house so as to unlock monies. Alternatively the son could become insolvent and his trustee in bankruptcy press for a sale;

(3) if the occupier is to have a stake in the property how are the respective interests to be dealt with during the 'repayment of discount period', and thereafter? and

(4) who is to pay the outgoings such as insurance and cost of
     repairs?

Of the precedents that follow, Precedent 19 recognises the contributor's stake and after repayment of that, splits the balance (say) 50/50
between the owner and the contributor. The precedent can easily be
adapted (in the Schedule) to recognise an amount that the owner
may have paid by varying the percentage due to the contributor.

Precedent 20 deals with a case where a mortgage is effected and
discharged by the former council tenant. It must be agreed how this
is to affect the interests of the parties; as drafted the contributor
benefits as the mortgage is reduced thus to an extent compensating
him for money laid out on which he is getting no return.

Precedent 21 provides for the proceeds of sale (after repayment of
any discount) to be split between the owner's grandchild and the
contributor (ie the owner's grandchild gets some of the benefit of the
discount at the end of the day). The precedent therefore contains
additional provisions to cope with the appointment of trustees and
deal with the proceeds of sale in the event that the grandchild is a
minor at the relevant time—hence the additional precedent concerning an appointment of trustees (Precedent 22).

4   Recognition of another's contribution

It is not uncommon for a person to join a sole proprietor of a property and subsequently spend his or her own money improving or
extending it. Particularly if the parties are not married, the party
who has expended money ('the contributor') may wish to acquire a
formal interest in the property.

If the property is subject to a mortgage then to place the title into
the joint names of the parties will invariably require the consent of
the mortgagee, and the contributor will be expected to covenant in
favour of the mortgagee. Costs will be involved.

Similarly, a property may have been purchased in one name
(because a spouse or partner was not available or did not want to be
involved in any mortgage application) and it is necessary to recognise the contributor's share or contribution. The transfer or conveyance into joint names will incur costs and if there is a mortgagee
involved require the mortgagee's consent and satisfaction of other
conditions.

It is simpler and cheaper that the property remain in the name of the sole proprietor. The following points should also be borne in mind.

(a)   Unregistered land

The proprietor should execute a declaration of trust to the effect that the property is held in specified shares for the proprietor and the contributor. Because the declaration will not affect the legal title, a caution against first registration should also be lodged (see above, p 51).

(b)   Registered land

The registered owner should execute a declaration of trust as above, and a restriction should be entered so that as sole proprietor the registered owner cannot dispose without the consent of the contributor or his personal representatives. Precedents 23 and 24 can be adapted to either registered or unregistered land.

5   Transfer of entire beneficial ownership

In contrast to the earlier section where property stood in the name of one person who wished to recognise the contribution or entitlement of another, there are cases where the sole owner wishes the entire beneficial entitlement to be transferred to another, but is unable to transfer/convey the legal estate without difficulty or expense. A typical situation would be where a husband owns a house subject to mortgage in his sole name and wishes to put it into his wife's names. This can involve a heavy liability to stamp duty.

If on a conveyance or transfer of property subject to a debt (and not a transfer of property in connection with divorce under Finance Act 1985, s 83(1)) the transferee covenants (either in the transfer or separately) to pay the debt or indemnify the transferor in respect thereof, such a covenant constitutes valuable consideration and establishes the transaction as a sale for stamp duty purposes. (Inland Revenue Statement of Practice, SP6/90 dated 27 April 1990).

Where no express covenant is given by the transferee the Revenue takes the view that one is implied unless a contrary intention is shown. Thus, unless s 83 above applies, a mortgaged property trans-ferred from one person to another will incur a charge to stamp duty unless it is clear that the transferor alone remains liable for the debt. This is unlikely if there is a transfer of the legal estate, for the mort-gagee will in most cases be taking a covenant from the transferee. It is appropriate therefore that legal title and the mortgage liability remain with the transferor, the equity in effect moving across via a declaration of trust (see Precedent 26).

Of course, the donee's position should be protected in the case of registered land by the registration of a restriction (see for example Precedent 25).

6   Steps to be taken

(a)   Stamp Duty

The declaration of trust will be stampable 50p.

(b)   HM Land Registry

The entry of a restriction on the register will cost £40.

(c)   Copies

All interested parties in the declaration of trust should have a copy

PRECEDENTS

Precedent 18—property purchased by nominee for person providing the purchase money.

THIS DECLARATION OF TRUST is made the   day of   19
BETWEEN (1) [X] of   [address] ('the Trustee') and (2) [Y]
of   [address] ('the Owner')

WHEREAS:

(A) By a conveyance dated   made between (1) [Vendor]
and (2) the Trustee the Property ('the Property') details of which are
given in the Schedule was conveyed to the Trustee

(B) The entirety of the purchase monies mentioned in the Conveyance
and the costs relating to the Conveyance were provided by the Owner

(C) Since the date of the Conveyance the Property has been held by
the Trustee as trustee for the Owner

NOW THIS DEED WITNESSES as follows:

1 The Trustee hereby DECLARES that he holds the Property UPON
TRUST for the Owner absolutely and that he will convey the Property
to the Owner or to such other person or persons as the Owner shall
direct and otherwise deal with the Property as the Owner shall direct.

2 The Owner hereby COVENANTS with the Trustee to indemnify him
against any costs properly incurred by the Trustee in relation to the
Property

   IN WITNESS etc

SCHEDULE

[description of Property]

Attestation—[as Precedent 1]

Precedent 19—council house: monies provided by third party to enable purchase by existing tenant. Split of 'profit' in agreed shares after repayment of discount. No mortgage.

THIS DECLARATION OF TRUST is made the   day of   19
BETWEEN:

(1)   of   ('the Owner') and (2)   of ('the Contributor')

1 Interpretation
In this Deed the following expressions shall have the following meanings:

1.1	'the Act'	means the Housing Act 1985 and any statutory modification or re-enactment thereof
1.2	'the Council'	means Borough Council
1.3	'the Property'	means ALL THAT freehold property situate at and known as [*insert address*]
1.4	'the Value'	means the sum of £ being the market value of the Property assessed in accordance with s127 of the Act
1.5	'the Discount'	means the sum of £ being the Discount to which the Owner is entitled under s129 of the Act
1.6	'the Discounted Purchase Price'	means the sum of £ paid by the Owner for the Property being the Value less the Discount
1.7	'the Contribution'	means the sum of £ paid by the Contributor as a contribution to the Discounted Purchase Price
18.	'Relevant Disposal'	means a disposal of the Property falling within sub-section (2) of s155 of the Act and giving rise to a repayment of the whole or part of the Discount
1.9	'the Relevant Discount'	shall mean a) in the first year from the date of the Conveyance a sum equal to the Discount b) in the second year from the date of the Conveyance a sum equal to two thirds of the Discount c) in the third year from the date of the Conveyance a sum equal to one third of the Discount

1.10 'the Conveyance'

    d) in the fourth and subsequent years from the date of the Conveyance a sum equal to nil

means a Conveyance of even date but executed before these presents made between (1) the Council and (2) the Owner

1.11 'the Net Proceeds of Sale' means the proceeds of sale of the Property together with the net rents and profits thereof until sale after deducting therefrom the costs of such sale.

2 Recitals

2.1 By the Conveyance the Property was conveyed to the Owner for an estate in fee simple in consideration of payment of the Discounted Purchase Price

2.2 The Conveyance contained a covenant on the part of the Owner to pay to the Council on demand an amount equal to the Relevant Discount if within a period of three years from the date of the Conveyance there is a Relevant Disposal but if there is more than one such disposal then only on the first of them

2.3 In view of the Contribution the parties have agreed that the Property and the Net Proceeds of Sale shall be held by the Owner upon trust for the Owner and the Contributor in manner mentioned below

3 IT IS HEREBY DECLARED that with effect from this date the Owner holds the Property UPON TRUST to sell the same and to stand possessed of the Net Proceeds of Sale in trust to divide the same between the Owner and the Contributor on the basis that:

3.1 the Contributor is entitled to the share of the Net Proceeds of Sale in accordance with the formula set out in the Schedule

3.2 the Owner is entitled to the balance of the Net Proceeds of Sale after deduction of the share of the Contributor above

4 IT IS HEREBY AGREED that

4.1 The Owner shall be entitled to occupy the Property rent free for as long as she shall wish and that the power of sale shall not be exercised without her consent.

4.2 During such occupation the Owner shall keep the Property in a reasonable state of repair and condition and shall insure the same for not less than the Value against damage by fire and other risks normally insured against and under a policy of insurance in respect of a private dwelling-house.

4.3 During such occupation the Owner shall not allow any person to share occupation of the Property upon terms that would enable any tenancy or security of tenure or interest in the Property or its proceeds of sale to be obtained by such person.

IN WITNESS whereof this deed has been duly executed the day and year first before written

SCHEDULE

The share of the net proceeds of sale of the Contributor shall be ascertained by

i)   taking the net proceeds of sale and

ii) in the first second or third year from the date of the Conveyance deducting therefrom the Relevant Discount and

iii) then taking off an amount equivalent to the Contribution and paying that to the Contributor (or if there are not sufficient monies to equal the Contribution the balance remaining) and holding [50%] of the balance for the Contributor.

SIGNED and DELIVERED AS
A DEED by the Owner in
the presence of:

SIGNED and DELIVERED AS
A DEED by the Contributor
in the presence of:

Precedent 20—council house: monies provided by Contributor to enable purchase by existing tenant. Split of 'profit' in agreed shares after repayment of discount. Mortgage granted to existing tenant who remains responsible for same.

THIS DECLARATION OF TRUST is made the   day of   19
BETWEEN: (1)   of   ('the Owner') and (2)
of   ('the Contributor')

1 Interpretation
In this deed the following expressions shall have the following meanings:
[*take in Precedent 19, clauses 1.1 to 1.10 inclusive*]

1.11 'the Net Proceeds of Sale'	means the proceeds of sale of the Property together with the net rents and profits thereof until sale after deducting therefrom the costs of such sale, and after repayment of the Mortgage
1.12 'the Mortgage'	means the sum secured by a Legal Charge over the Property in favour of [*Building Society*] being originally £ or such sum from time to time outstanding thereunder

2 Recitals
[*as Precedent 19, clause 2*]

3 IT IS HEREBY DECLARED that with effect from this date the Owner holds the Property Subject to the Mortgage UPON TRUST to sell the same and to stand possessed of the Net Proceeds of Sale in trust to divide the same between the Owner and the Contributor on the basis that:
3.1 the Contributor is entitled to the share of the Net Proceeds of Sale in accordance with the formula set out in the Schedule
3.2 the Owner is entitled to the balance of the Net Proceeds of Sale after deduction of the share of the Contributor above

4 IT IS HEREBY AGREED that
4.1 The Owner shall be entitled to occupy the Property rent free for so long as she shall wish and that the power of sale shall not be exercised without her consent.
4.2 During such occupation the Owner shall not allow any person to share occupation of the Property upon terms that would enable any tenancy or security of tenure or interest in the Property or its proceeds of sale to be obtained by such person.
4.3 The Owner shall be liable to make all payments due under the Mortgage and shall observe the terms and conditions thereof and indemnifies the Contributor accordingly.

IN WITNESS whereof this deed has been duly executed the day and year first before written

SCHEDULE

The share of the net proceeds of sale of the Contributor shall be ascertained by

i)   taking the net proceeds of sale and

ii) in the first second or third year from the date of the Conveyance deducting therefrom the Relevant Discount and

iii) then taking off an amount equivalent to the Contribution and paying that to the Contributor (or if there are not sufficient monies to equal the Contribution the balance remaining) and

iv) holding [50%] of the balance for the Contributor.

SIGNED and DELIVERED AS
A DEED by the Owner in the
presence of:

SIGNED and DELIVERED AS
A DEED by the Contributor
in the presence of:

**Precedent 21—council house: monies provided by third party.
Benefit of occupier's share held for grandchildren.**

THIS DECLARATION OF TRUST is made the   day of   19
BETWEEN: (1)   of   ('the Owner') and (2)
of   ('the Contributor')

1 Interpretation
In this deed the following expressions shall have the following meanings:
[*take in Precedent 19 clauses 1.1 to 1.11 inclusive*]

2 Recitals
2.1 [Precedent 19 clause 2.1]
2.2 [Precedent 19 clause 2.2]
2.3 The parties have agreed that the Property and the Net Proceeds of Sale shall be held by the Owner upon the trusts set out hereafter.

3 IT IS HEREBY DECLARED that with effect from this date the Owner holds the Property UPON TRUST to sell the same and to stand possessed of the Net Proceeds of Sale on the basis that:
3.1 the Contributor Is entitled to the share of the Net Proceeds of Sale in accordance with the formula set out in the Schedule
3.2 the balance thereof shall be held for X and Y (being the grandchildren of the Owner) in equal shares

4 [Precedent 19 clause 4]

5 IT IS HEREBY AGREED AND DECLARED by the parties hereto that the power of appointing new Trustees of this Deed shall be vested in [the Contributor]

6 ALL monies liable to be invested under the trusts and provisions hereof may be invested at the absolute discretion of the Trustees hereof in the purchase or acquisition of and at interest upon such shares stocks funds securities or other investments of whatever nature or wheresoever situate and whether producing income or not whether involving liability or not as the Trustees shall in their absolute discretion think fit to the intent that the Trustees shall have the same full and unrestricted powers of investing and varying investments in all respects as if they were absolutely and beneficially entitled thereto

7 THE statutory powers of maintenance accumulation and advancement shall apply to the trusts declared herein but so that the power of maintenance shall be exercisable as the Trustees shall think fit and free from any obligation to apply a proportionate part only of income where other income is applicable for maintenance purposes and the power of advancement shall authorise the application of the whole or any part (instead of being limited to one half) of the share or interest of a beneficiary hereunder

8 IN the event that any of the persons named in clause 3.2 hereof shall be an infant the Trustee shall have power to pay any monies to which such infant is entitled to the parent or guardian of such infant whose receipt shall be a good discharge to the Trustees

IN WITNESS etc

SCHEDULE

[as Precedent 19]

SIGNED and DELIVERED
as a DEED by the Owner
in the presence of:

SIGNED and DELIVERED
as a DEED by the
Contributor in the
presence of:

Precedent 22—retirement of council occupier as trustee of the Declaration.

THIS DEED OF RETIREMENT AND APPOINTMENT OF NEW TRUSTEES is made this   day of   19
BETWEEN: (1) [*The Owner*]   of   ('the Retiring Trustee') (2) [*The Contributor and parent of grandchild*] of   ('the New Trustees')

WHEREAS:

(A) By a Declaration of Trust ('the Declaration') dated   and made by the Retiring Trustee and the [*Contributor*] trusts were declared concerning the Property described in the Schedule and the net proceeds of sale thereof

(B) By the Declaration the power of appointing new trustees of it was vested in the Contributor

(C) The Retiring Trustee wishes to be discharged from the trusts of the Declaration

(D) The Contributor wishes to appoint the New Trustees to be trustees of the trusts of the Declaration in place of the Retiring Trustee

NOW THIS DEED WITNESSES that in exercise of the power in that behalf vested in him by the Declaration and of every other power him enabling the Contributor APPOINTS the New Trustees to be trustees of the Declaration in the place of the Retiring Trustee who hereby retires.

IN WITNESS etc

SCHEDULE

[*description of the Property*]

Attestation—[*as Precedent 1*]

Precedent 23—property in sole name of one party subject to mortgage. Declaration of trust that property held for self and another in specified shares.

THIS DECLARATION OF TRUST is made this   day of   19
BETWEEN (1) [X] of   [address] ('Legal Owner') and (2) [Y]
of   [address] ('the Contributor')

WHEREAS:

(A) By a Transfer dated   the property ('the Property')
details of which are contained in the Schedule was transferred to the
Legal Owner

(B) By a Mortgage ('the Mortgage') dated the same date as the transfer the Legal Owner charged the Property to the [Building Society] to
secure the sum of £

(C) The purchase money for the Property was provided by the Legal
Owner and the Contributor in the shares and proportions hereinafter
mentioned and the Property was transferred to the Legal Owner who
confirms that he holds the same as trustee for himself and the
Contributor

NOW THIS DEED WITNESSES as follows:

1 The Legal Owner declares that he holds the Property in trust for
himself and the Contributor in fee simple

2 The Legal Owner and the Contributor hereby declare that the income
from the Property and the proceeds of sale thereof (after deducting
thereout the cost of sale but not the balance of any money due under
the Mortgage) shall be held by them upon trust to divide the same into
[56] equal parts and to stand possessed of:

   [41] such equal parts thereof for the Legal Owner

   [15] equal parts thereof for the Contributor

3 The Legal Owner charges his said shares in the Property with the
payment of all monies secured by the Mortgage in exoneration of the
Contributor's shares in the Property

4 The Legal Owner hereby covenants with the Contributor that he will
pay all monies secured by and payable under the Mortgage and will
at all times hereafter indemnify and keep indemnified the Contributor
and his estate and effects from all actions proceedings costs claims
and demands in respect thereof

5 The Legal Owner hereby covenants with the Contributor that he will
not create any further mortgages or otherwise deal with or dispose of
all or any part of the Property without the consent in writing of the
Contributor

IN WITNESS etc

SCHEDULE

[particulars of Property]

Attestation—*[as Precedent 1]*

Precedent 24—property in sole name of wife subject to mortgage. Declaration of trust recognises the contribution of husband by way of improvements to the property. Power of sale limited during lifetime of survivor.

THIS DECLARATION OF TRUST is made this   day of   19
BY   of   ('the Owner') and to which [*the Contributor*] ('(the Contributor') of   is a party to show his acceptance of the terms hereof

WHEREAS:

A The Owner is the registered proprietor of the property ('the Property') details of which are contained in the Schedule

B SINCE the acquisition of the Property in her then name of the Owner has married the Contributor

C The Contributor has expended substantial monies on the Property and it is agreed between the Owner and the Contributor that the Property (subject to the existing Mortgage in favour of [*Building Society*]) should be held as to three-fifths for the Owner and two-fifths for the Contributor or their respective Estates

NOW IT IS HEREBY DECLARED as follows:

1 The Owner declares that she holds the Property and the net proceeds of sale thereof as to three-fifths for herself and two-fifths for the Contributor

2 IT is agreed between the Owner and the Contributor that any Mortgage on the Property should be deducted from the net proceeds of sale before any division thereof

3 IT is agreed between the Owner and the Contributor that neither of them nor their respective personal representatives can force a sale of the Property during the lifetime of either of them

4 IT is agreed that a restriction will be registered at HM Land Registry to the effect that the Owner cannot sell the Property without the consent of the Contributor during his lifetime or the consent of his personal representatives following his death

5 IT is agreed between the Owner and the Contributor that this Declaration shall be binding upon their respective Personal Representatives

IN WITNESS whereof the Owner and the Contributor have duly executed this Deed the day and year first before written

SCHEDULE

[*description of Property*]

Attestation—[*as Precedent 1*]

Precedent 25—application to register a Restriction under section 58 of the 1925 Act.

Form 75

HM LAND REGISTRY

Land Registration Acts 1925 to 1986

County and district
Title Number(s)
Property

[*The Owner*] (name and address as per Charge Certificate)

hereby applies to the registrar to enter the following restriction against the title(s) above mentioned:

Restriction—Except under an order of the registrar, no disposition by the proprietor(s) of the land is to be registered without the consent of [name and address of the Contributor] during his lifetime or his personal representatives after his death

Signature of applicant
or his Solicitor(s)

Date

Address of solicitor(s)

Solicitors reference   Telephone No

Precedent 26—house in sole name, subject to mortgage. Equity henceforward held for another. Transferor remaining liable on mortgage.

THIS DEED OF TRUST is made the   day of   19
BETWEEN (1) [X] of   [address] ('the Trustee') and (2) [Y]
of   [address] ('the Beneficiary')

WHEREAS:

(A) The Trustee is the registered proprietor of the property ('the Property') details of which are given in the schedule hereto Subject to a charge ('the Registered Charge') in favour of [National Westminster Home Loans Limited]

(B) The Trustee is desirous of holding the Property Subject to the Registered Charge UPON TRUST for [Y] absolutely

NOW THIS DEED WITNESSES as follows:

1 The Trustee hereby DECLARES that henceforward he holds the Property Subject to the Registered Charge UPON TRUST for the beneficiary absolutely and that he will sell transfer assign or otherwise deal with the Property as the Beneficiary shall direct Subject always to the provisions of the Registered Charge

2 The Trustee hereby covenants with the Beneficiary that he will continue to pay all monthly and other payments for which he is liable under the Registered Charge

IN WITNESS etc

SCHEDULE

[description of Property]

Attestation—[as Precedent 1]

5

Insurance policies

1 Introduction

It is not unusual for an insurance policy to be taken out under trusts *ab initio*, for instance written under the Married Women's Property Act 1882 for the benefit of a spouse, or more usually for the benefit of children to provide monies for inheritance tax purposes. However, it is also not unusual for a policy holder to have effected a policy on his own life for his own benefit (for instance an endowment policy which might have been taken out with a maturity date to coincide with expected payment of school fees or merely as a savings vehicle) and for that policy then to become surplus to requirements. Certainly there seems little point these days in an elderly client retaining a Whole Life with Profits policy in his own estate.

There are two ways of dealing with such policies:

1   they can be assigned by the policyholder by way of gift (or even by way of sale if money needs to be raised) to a named beneficiary or to trustees; Law of Property Act 1925, s 136 (see Precedents in *Encyclopedia of Forms and Precedents* (5th edn, Butterworths), Vol 20, p 534); or

2   the policyholder can declare that he holds the policy upon trusts as set out in a declaration of trust (see Precedent 27). Obviously in this latter case the policyholder becomes the sole trustee and it would be sensible to have a deed of appointment of trustees as soon as possible following the declaration of trust so that there are outside trustees available to claim the policy proceeds at the appropriate time (see Precedents 28 and 32).

2 The contents of the declaration of trust/assignment

(a) Bonuses/Profits

It is presumed in all cases that the settlor would wish to settle not only the sum assured but all bonuses and profits accruing thereto. Often the most valuable portion of policy proceeds is the terminal bonus where a policy is one of long standing.

(b) Debts

The policy may already be charged (sometimes in favour of the insurance company itself to secure a loan) and it is important to be clear whether the settlement of the policy is to be subject to the debt or whether this is to be paid by the settlor or his estate, thus reimbursing the trustees at maturity (as the chargee will already have helped himself from the policy proceeds!).

(c) Payment of premiums

In a voluntary settlement it would not be usual for the settlor donor to covenant to continue to pay any premiums. After all, the beauty of policies taken out for IHT purposes is that the settlor has the flexibility of discontinuing payment of the premiums if circumstances change (the policy becoming either paid up or the donees themselves paying the premiums). However, it is useful to have an acknowledgement that any premiums paid by the settlor do not create a lien in his favour for the same.

(d) Covenant for title

The covenants for title that we associate with real property conveyances and transfers are not limited to land alone (Law of Property Act 1925, s 76 and definition in s 205). From 1 July 1995 the Law of Property (Miscellaneous Provisions) Act 1994 introduced covenants 'with full title guarantee' or 'with limited title guarantee'. Covenants are only implied if the key words are used. As the circumstances envisaged here are those of gift, it is inappropriate for any covenants to be implied (see further Aldridge, *Implied Covenants for Title* FT Law & Tax, 1995).

(e)   Covenant not to render the policy void

Such a covenant would be normal in a commercial assignment (eg on a matrimonial division of assets), but would not usually be included in a voluntary situation. However, if included, and the settlor for instance takes up motor racing in breach of the terms of the policy, then there would be a right of action by the trustees against him or his estate (*Re Jewell's Settlement, Watts v Public Trustee* [1919] 2 Ch 161).

(f)   Powers

It is always prudent for trustees to have power to surrender the policy and deal generally with it so that they have maximum flexibility of action to cope with unanticipated events (for instance power to convert the policy to be paid up should the settlor cease to pay premiums, or power to lodge the policy by way of security for a loan to a beneficiary).

3   Retirement annuity policies

These policies, taken out under Income and Corporation Taxes Act 1970, s 226 (replaced by ICTA 1988, s 620) and no longer available after July 1988, are most valuable policies.

1   they enable the self-employed to make provision for a pension out of income; subject to the limits on contribution, such contributions are wholly deductible for tax purposes from the payer's income. The limits on contribution are limited to a percentage of the eligible income but there is no 'capping' as in the case for an employee in a company pension scheme;

2   they allow a tax–free lump sum of up to three times the annual amount of the gross annuity that can be secured by the balance of the fund (subject to a maximum sum of £150,000 where the policy was set up after 17 March 1987) to be taken at the time of commencement of the pension.

It will be appreciated that the value of such a policy could be considerable. In the event of death before retirement and depending upon the exact terms of the policy, the value of the policy fund could become payable to the policyholder's estate. Thus, in the case of a single man for instance the fund would (subject to the estate exceeding £154,000) be subject to inheritance tax. It is prudent to arrange for this death benefit to fall outside the policyholder's estate. Because the right to the annuity and the death benefit comprise a single chose in action, it is not possible to assign the death benefit alone. The policyholder should declare himself trustee of both elements (and appoint additional trustees) with the advantage that:

1   the death benefit payment can be made to trustees of the policy without the necessity of having to wait for a grant of probate to the policyholder's estate; and

2   if at the time of declaring the trust the policyholder is in normal health for his age, it is understood that the Revenue will treat the gift as a nominal transfer of value for IHT purposes. This treatment rests upon correspondence between the Revenue and the Association of British Insurers and indications from the Capital Taxes Office (see Tolley's *Inheritance Tax 1994/95*) so cannot be regarded as absolutely conclusive. On the other hand there would not appear to be any fiscal disadvantage in dealing with the policy in this way.

It is likely therefore that if a policyholder in a state of serious ill-health settles an existing policy, the Revenue may wish to raise a claim for IHT, particularly if larger than usual premiums were subsequently paid into the policy (see IHTA 1984, s 3(3)).

As assignment of retirement annuities is not allowed, it is best to establish the trust by way of declaration and then appoint a further trustee in the deed itself or by separate deed. In effect, if the policyholder lives to normal retirement age and commences to draw a pension, then the trust is of no value.

The disadvantages are:

1   once the beneficiaries are named, it is not possible to change them

2   once a trustee is appointed it is not possible to remove him (other than in the circumstances set out in Trustee Act 1925, s 36).

The precedents that follow either:

1   settle the death benefit of the policy for named beneficiaries (Precedent 30); or

2   settle the death benefit of the policy upon discretionary trusts on the basis that an appointment of the trust fund is made within two years of the policyholder's death (Precedent 31).

4   Personal pension contracts

These are the successors to retirement annuity contracts for the self-employed (see Income and Corporation Taxes Act 1988, Chap IV, Pt XIV). The main advantage is that a pension can be drawn at any time after the age of 50 (whereas retirement annuity contract pensions cannot be drawn before the age of 60 unless there is retirement on the grounds of ill-health).

It was thought by most insurance companies (for instance Scottish Widows) that as they were the scheme administrator in respect of such policies, then in the absence of a specific trust, the insurance company would have a discretion as to how to distribute any lump sum payable on death before retirement and that, as such, any payment would not be liable to inheritance tax. The insurance company would anticipate being guided by an expression of wishes from the policyholder (similar to a company death in service scheme). It is understood that the Inland Revenue have challenged this view, and that discussions (May 1995) are in progress between the Association of British Insurers and the Capital Taxes Office.

As such it would appear that simplicity and flexibility provided by an expression of wishes are not presently available (it was always very easy to change an expression of wishes), but that the death benefit payable prior to retirement if under trust should avoid a charge to IHT. As is the case of retirement annuities, there seems no fiscal disadvantage in dealing with the policy in this way. However, as personal pension policies seem to be written in different ways by different companies, it is as well to check with the companies concerned before embarking on the settlement of such policies. In the circumstances no suggested precedent is included here.

5 Steps to be taken following the declaration or assignment

(a) Stamp Duty

A declaration of trust is stampable 50p. An assignment by way of gift will not be stampable if it contains the appropriate exemption certificate, viz:

'It is certified that this instrument falls within Category L in The Schedule to The Stamp Duty (Exempt Instruments) Regulations 1987.'

The deed of appointment of new trustees (Precedents 28 and 32) are not subject to Stamp Duty (Finance Act 1991, s 110).

(b) Notice of assignment (Precedent 29)

No assignee of a life policy can sue an insurance company for policy monies until notice of assignment has been given and such notice should specify the date and purpose of the assignment (Policies of Assurance Act 1867, s 3). Notice of the declaration and appointment of trustees or of the assignment should therefore be given to the insurance company—in practice it is found that they do now require to see (and sometimes retain) the original documents.

PRECEDENTS

Precedent 27—Declaration of trust of life policy by way of gift for benefit of children.

THIS DECLARATION OF TRUST is made this   day of   19
by [name] of   [address] ('the Settlor')

WHEREAS:

(A) The Settlor is the beneficial owner of the Policy ('the Policy') details of which are given in the Schedule hereto

(B) The Settlor wishes to settle the Policy for the benefit of his children (all of whom are of full age) as herein appears

NOW IT IS HEREBY DECLARED as follows:

1 Henceforth the Settlor HOLDS the Policy and all monies assured by or to become payable thereunder and all benefits and advantages thereof (or any policy or policies substituted for the same) UPON TRUST for his children X Y and Z in equal shares absolutely.

2 The Settlor acknowledges that in so far as he pays any further premium in respect of the Policy he claims no lien on the Policy in respect of such payment.

3 It is hereby certified that this instrument falls within Category L in the Schedule to the Stamp Duty (Exempt Instruments) Regulations 1987.

   IN WITNESS whereof this deed has been duly executed the day and year before written

SCHEDULE

Life Assured   [The Settlor]
Policy No
Assurance Company
Sum Assured
When payable
Date of Policy
Premium   [per month/per annum]

SIGNED and DELIVERED
as a DEED by the Settlor
in the presence of:

Precedent 28—Deed of Appointment of Trustees of a Declaration of Trust. Settlor ceasing to be a trustee.

THIS DEED OF APPOINTMENT AND RETIREMENT is made this day of   19

BETWEEN:

(1) [*The Settlor*] of   [*address*] ('the Appointor') and

(2) X of   [*address*] Y of   [*address*] and Z of [*address*] ('the New Trustees')

WHEREAS:

(A) The Appointor is the sole trustee of a Declaration of Trust dated   ('the Declaration') made by the Appointor in relation to a Policy details of which are given in the Schedule hereto

(B) The Appointor wishes to appoint the New Trustees to be trustees of the Declaration and himself to retire as a trustee thereof

NOW THIS DEED WITNESSES that in exercise of the power given to him by the Trustee Act 1925 and of every other power him enabling the Appointor hereby APPOINTS the New Trustees to be trustees of the Declaration in place of the Appointor who hereby retires as a trustee thereof

IN WITNESS etc

SCHEDULE

[*take in details of the Policy from Declaration*]

Attestation by all parties

Precedent 29—Notice of Declaration of Trust and Appointment of Trustees to Assurance Company.

To [*Assurance Company—name and address*]

    Policy No [   ]

    Life Assured [   ]

As Solicitors for and on behalf of X Y and Z we hereby give you notice that:

(a) by a Declaration of Trust dated   made by [*Settlor*] the above policy was declared to be subject to the trusts thereof

(b) by a Deed of Appointment and Retirement dated [   ] X Y and Z were appointed trustees of the Declaration and [*Settlor*] retired as a trustee thereof

A copy certified by us to be a true copy of each document referred to above is enclosed.

Pleace acknowledge receipt by signing and returning the duplicate of this notice enclosed.

Dated [*insert date*]

Signed [*insert name and address of Solicitors*]

Precedent 30—declaration of trust and assignment (coupled with an appointment of trustees) of retirement annuity policy. Definite beneficiaries. Wide trust powers to cover possibility of minority beneficiaries.

THIS DECLARATION OF TRUST AND ASSIGNMENT is made the day of   19
BETWEEN:

(1) *[Policy holder's full name and address]* ('the Settlor') and

(2) the Settlor and   of   and   of ('the Trustees' which expression shall include the trustee or trustees for the time being hereof)

WHEREAS:

(A) The Settlor is the beneficial owner of certain benefits provided for under the policy or policies approved under Section 620 and/or Section 621 of the Income and Corporation Taxes Act 1988 further details of which are given in the Schedule hereto ('the Policy' which term is more particularly defined in Clause 1)

(B) The Settlor wishes to settle the Policy and the Trustees have agreed to take an assignment thereof to hold the same upon the trusts and with and subject to the powers and provisions set out below

NOW THIS DEED WITNESSES as follows:

1 In this Declaration the following expressions shall have the following meanings:

    (a) 'the Policy' shall mean the policy mentioned above and in the Schedule hereto or any other policy or policies for the time being subject to the trusts hereof including any policy accepted by the Trustees by way of further settlement or issued in exchange or in substitution for any policy or otherwise being a policy or policies in a form approved by the Board of Inland Revenue pursuant to section 620 and/or section 621 of the Income and Corporation Taxes Act 1988 or any statutory modification re-enactment or replacement thereof and 'Policies' shall have a corresponding meaning.

    (b) 'the Individual Pension' shall mean all the rights and provisions which may accrue and monies which may become payable under the Policy but excluding the Spouse's or Dependant's Annuity and the Death Benefit.

    (c) 'the Spouse's or Dependant's Annuity' shall mean any annuity or annuities payable under the Policy and stated to be payable to the Settlor's Spouse or other defined Dependant.

    (d) 'the Death Benefit' shall mean any monies payable under the Policy in the event of the death of the Settlor otherwise than in the form of an annuity or lump sum arising from the

commutation of an annuity and all capital sums or investments held by the Trustees representing such benefits for
the time being.

2 The Settlor hereby DECLARES himself to be trustee of the policy and
IRREVOCABLY ASSIGNS the Policy to the Trustees (who hereby
acknowledge receipt of the same) to hold the same on the trusts and
with and subject to the powers and provisions set out herein.

3 The Settlor ACKNOWLEDGES that he alone is entitled to make
payment of any future premiums under the Policy (but does not
thereby undertake any obligation to pay the same) and claims no lien
in respect of any such payments.

4 The Trustees shall hold the Individual Pension upon trust for the
absolute benefit of the Settlor.

5 The Trustees shall hold the Spouse's or Dependant's Annuity upon
trust absolutely for the person or persons named in the Policy and sat-
isfying the conditions contained or referred to in the Policy.

6 The Trustees shall hold the Death Benefit upon trust for the benefit
of [*insert named beneficiaries*].

7 All income accruing in the hands of the Trustees whether before or
after the death of the Settlor shall be paid or applied to or for the
benefit of the individual(s) entitled for the time being to such income
under the trusts hereof.

8 In addition to the powers conferred by law the Trustees shall have
the following powers in the execution of these Trusts:
  (a) power to invest or apply any monies requiring investment
      in such investments of whatever nature whether income
      producing or non income producing and whether or not
      authorised by law for the investment of trust funds includ-
      ing life assurance policies (whether unit linked or not) as the
      Trustees in their absolute discretion think fit with a like
      power of carrying such investments to the intent that the
      Trustees shall have the same full and unrestricted powers
      of investment or variation of investment as if they were
      absolute owners beneficially entitled including the power to
      lend money to the executors and trustees of the Settlor's
      Will with or without security upon such terms as they may
      think fit and so that the Trustees shall not be liable for any
      loss which may occur at any time in connection with or in
      consequence of any investments made under the powers
      hereby conferred upon them
  (b) power during the minority of a beneficiary to pay or apply
      the income or capital to which such beneficiary may be
      entitled for or towards the advancement maintenance edu-
      cation or benefit of such beneficiary (without regard to limits

otherwise imposed by statute) and to make such payments to the parents or guardians of such beneficiary for the purposes aforesaid without seeing to the application thereof and so that the receipt of such parents or guardians shall be a complete discharge to the Trustees;

(c)　power to cause any property for the time being subject to the foregoing trusts to be registered in the name or names of or to be held under the control of any other person or persons whatsoever as nominees and to pay any expenses in connection therewith out of capital or income as the Trustees may consider proper BUT SO THAT the Trustees shall not be liable for any loss which may be occasioned by the use of this power.

9 The Trustees shall exercise all the rights and options contained in or allowed in connection with the Policy in such manner as the Settlor shall from time to time direct in writing to the Trustees and notwithstanding that the Settlor may be one of the Trustees his right to give directions shall not be a fiduciary right but shall be exercisable by him without reference to any trust and such powers shall be exercisable by him without reference or regard to the trusts hereby declared.

10 Neither the Settlor nor any other of the Trustees shall be under any obligation whatsoever to keep up the Policy or to reinstate the same if it shall become void.

11 Any Trustee (other than the Settlor) hereof being a solicitor or other person engaged in any profession or business shall be entitled to be paid all usual professional or other charges for business transacted time expended and acts done by him or his firm in connection with the trusts hereof including acts which a Trustee not being in any profession or business could have done personally.

12 (i)　The power of appointing new or additional trustees hereof shall be vested in the Settlor during his lifetime

(ii)　Any corporate body may be appointed trustee hereof on such terms and conditions as to remuneration and otherwise in all respects as the appointor shall prescribe or approve.

13 In the performance of the trusts hereof no trustee shall be liable for any loss arising as a result of any act done or omission made in good faith or by reason of any mistake made by that trustee (other than a mistake which amounts to culpable wrongdoing on the part of that trustee).

14 The Trustees may at any time or times during the continuance of the trusts hereof by deed or deeds release or restrict the future exercise of all or any of the powers herein conferred on them either wholly and so as to bind their successors or to any lesser extent specified in any such deed or deeds.

15 We hereby certify that this instrument falls within category L in the Schedule to the Stamp Duty (Exempt Instruments) Regulations 1987.

IN WITNESS etc

SCHEDULE

Policy No(s)
Assurance Company
Date of policy(ies)

SIGNED and delivered as a
Deed by the Settlor in
the presence of:

SIGNED and delivered as a
Deed by [Trustee] in the
presence of:

SIGNED and delivered as a
Deed by [Trustee] in the
presence of

Precedent 31—Declaration of Trust of retirement annuity policies. Discretionary trust to be exercised within two years of death.

DECLARATION OF TRUST

THIS DECLARATION OF TRUST is made this   day of   19 BY [insert full name and address]

WHEREAS I have effected with the Companies listed in the Second Schedule hereto on my own life in pursuance of the provisions of section 620 of the Income and Corporation Taxes Act 1988 (or former enactments such as section 226 of the Income and Corporation Taxes Act 1970) the pension annuity policies (hereinafter together called 'the Policy') shortly described in the Second Schedule hereto

AND WHEREAS it is my desire to declare over the Policy such trusts as hereinafter appear and subject to the powers and provisions specified in the Trust Provisions and Trustee Powers set out in the First Schedule hereto

NOW I hereby DECLARE that I shall henceforward hold the Policy and the benefits payable thereunder upon trust as follows:

1 AS to any sum payable under the terms of the Policy in the event of my death before the Agreed Pension Date specified in the Policy (hereinafter called 'the Death Benefit') UPON TRUST for such one or more exclusively or all of the following class namely:

(i)   any person to whom I shall be or shall have been married
(ii)   any child or children of mine whenever born
(iii) any grandchild or grandchildren of mine whenever born
(iv) my parents [insert names]
(v)   any other individual (excluding myself) or charity nominated by myself by notice in writing addressed to and received by the Trustee not later than one month prior to my death

in such shares and for such interests whether absolute or limited as the Trustees shall in their uncontrolled discretion appoint during my lifetime or within the period of two years from the date of my death PROVIDED ALWAYS that any part of the Death Benefit which shall remain unappointed as aforesaid at the end of the said period of two years shall be held by the Trustees for such of my widow and children as are alive at that time and if more than one in equal shares but if the foregoing trusts shall fail then upon trust absolutely for such charity or charities as the Trustees shall in their absolute discretion select and for the general purposes of the same

2 AS to the Annuity payable to me on survival to the Agreed Pension Date UPON TRUST for myself absolutely

3 As to any annuity payable to the widow or other approved dependant pursuant to the exercise of any option incorporated in the Policy UPON TRUST for such annuitant absolutely

4 NO lien is claimed by me upon the Policy in respect of any future payment of premium

THE FIRST SCHEDULE
TRUST PROVISIONS AND TRUSTEE POWERS

1 THE trustee or trustees for the time being hereof (hereinafter called 'the Trustees') shall hold the Policy and all the monies which may become payable thereunder or under any substituted policy or policies including the accumulation of income from any such monies and the whole benefit of such Policy and all assets which may from time to time represent the same and all income derived therefrom upon the trusts hereinbefore declared

2 THE Death Benefit may be invested in such investments of whatever nature whether income producing or non income producing and whether or not authorised by law for the investment of trust funds including life assurance policies (whether unit linked or not) as the Trustees in their absolute discretion think fit with a like power of varying such investments to the intent that the Trustees shall have the same full and unrestricted powers of investment or variation of investment as if they were absolute owners beneficially entitled including the power to lend money to the executors and trustees of my Will with or without security upon such terms as they may think fit and so that the Trustees shall not be liable for any loss which may occur at any time in connection with or in consequence of any investments made under the powers hereby conferred upon them

3 THE Trustees shall have power during the minority of a beneficiary to pay or apply the income or capital to which such beneficiary may be entitled for or towards the advancement maintenance education or benefit of such beneficiary (without regard to limits otherwise imposed by statute) and to make such payments to the parents or guardians of such beneficiary for the purpose aforesaid without seeing to the application thereof and so that the receipt of such parents or guardian shall be a complete discharge to the Trustees

4 THE Trustees may appropriate any part of the Death Benefit in its actual state of investment and after making such valuations as the Trustees shall think fit in or towards the satisfaction of the interest of any person beneficially interested in the Death Benefit or the income thereof but without the necessity of obtaining the consent of that or of any other person

5 ANY trustee (other than myself) being a Solicitor or other person engaged in any profession or business shall be entitled to be paid all usual professional or other charges for business transacted time expended and acts done by him or his firm in connection with the

trusts hereof including acts which a trustee not being in any profession or business could have done personally

6 A corporate trustee may be appointed a trustee hereof on such terms and conditions as to remuneration and otherwise in all respects as shall be agreed at the time of appointment

7 THE Trustees may as they in their absolute discretion think fit pay or apply all or any part or parts of the Death Benefit in or towards the discharge of any liabilities to Inheritance Tax or other fiscal imposition arising by reason of my death and in respect of which the liability for such a payment would otherwise fall entirely either directly or indirectly on any one or more of the beneficiaries hereunder by reason of whatever interest any of them may have in any such property and which liability would otherwise diminish or otherwise affect their entitlement to such property PROVIDED that no such payment by the Trustees on behalf of any beneficiary as aforesaid shall exceed the value of the interest which such beneficiary has in the Death Benefit at the time of such payment by the Trustees whether absolute or contingent on any event or in possession or in remainder or in reversion

8 THE Trustees may accept as a good and sufficient discharge a receipt of the Treasurer or other proper officer of a charity to whom payment is made as a good and sufficient discharge for such payment

9 IN the professed execution and administration of the trusts hereof no Trustee shall be liable for any loss to the Death Benefit arising by reason of any investment made in good faith or by reason of any mistake or omission made in good faith made by any trustee or by reason of any other matter or thing except wilful and individual fraud or wrong doing on the part of the Trustee who is sought to be made liable

10 THE power of appointing new or additional trustees is vested in me during my lifetime

THE SECOND SCHEDULE

[insert details of policy/policies as Precedent 1]

IN WITNESS etc

SIGNED and
DELIVERED as a DEED by the said
[X] in the presence
of:

Precedent 32—deed of appointment of trustees of a Declaration of Trust. Settlor remaining as a trustee.

THIS DEED OF APPOINTMENT is made this   day of   19
BETWEEN
(1) [name and address of Declarer] ('the Appointor') and
(2) [name and address of additional trustees] ('the New Trustees')

WHEREAS:

(A) BY a Declaration of Trust ('the Declaration') dated   19
the Appointor declared that he held the policy/policies details of which
are given in the Schedule hereto upon the trusts and subject to the
powers and provisions as set out in the Declaration

(B) THE Appointor wishes to appoint the New Trustees to be Trustees
of the Declaration with himself

NOW THIS DEED WITNESSES that in exercise of the power given to
him by the Trustee Act 1925 and of the power given to him in the
Declaration the Appointor HEREBY APPOINTS the New Trustees to
be Trustees of the Declaration to act jointly with himself in the trusts
of the same

   IN WITNESS etc

[take in details of the Policy/ies from the Declaration]

Attestation

6

Company shareholdings

1 Introduction

Company shares, just like so many other assets, can be the subject of a trust. The company itself is not concerned with any trusts to which its shares may be subject (Companies Act 1985, s 360); the members shown on the register of shareholders are its members, whether or not they are trustees or nominees for another.

In the case of joint shareholdings, unless the Articles of Association specify otherwise, it is the first-named holder who has the vote. (The Companies (Tables A to F) Regulations 1985 (SI No 805), Table A, reg 55). If there is disagreement between joint shareholders as to how a vote should be exercised, that is not a matter which concerns the company.

As in all trusts there should be certainty as to the subject matter of the trust, otherwise it is void. Obviously if numbered shares are the subject of a trust, their identity is clear. However, the holding of a block of shares means that the shares are indistinguishable one from another. Provided that the proportion or number of shares is clear then a declaration of trust that a person is trustee for another of a proportion of the shares owned by the trustee is not void for lack of certainty (*Hunter v Moss* [1994] 1 WLR 452).

2 Shares in the subsidiary

Many companies have a subsidiary which has two shareholders, with one share (or the entire number of issued shares except for one) being held by the parent company and the remaining share being held either by the parent company and an individual (normally a director) or by the individual alone.

In such circumstances, to protect the parent company, it is appropriate that the individual shareholder should:

1   make a declaration of trust acknowledging that he holds the share for the parent company and will act in accordance with its instructions; and

2   sign a blank stock transfer form, so that the parent (who should also hold the share certificate) can transfer the shareholding at any appropriate time.

Because this is a bare trust, there is no need for the individual trustee shareholder to have any specific powers or duties. He must act as instructed by the parent company beneficiary. If further emphasis is needed, the provisions of Precedent 34 can be incorporated into Precedent 33.

It should of course be mentioned that since the coming into force on 15 July 1992 of the Companies (Single Member Private Limited Companies) Regulations 1992 (SI No 1699), only one member is required for a private limited liability company as opposed to the two members previously required under the provisions of the Companies Act 1985, s 24, which section rendered a sole shareholder (jointly and severally with the company) liable for its debts and liabilities.

3   The nominee/trustee shareholder

There are many reasons why shares may be held by the registered shareholder for someone else, whether in relation to all or part of the shareholding. The Companies Act 1985, Pt VI (as amended by the Companies Act 1989) and the Disclosure of Interests in Shares (Amendment) Regulations 1993 (SI No 1819) require a disclosure of underlying ownership so far as public companies are concerned, and it is not proposed to deal with that aspect here.

A declaration of trust relating to shares in a private company may be appropriate:

1   where a person wishes to be an anonymous shareholder or has purchased shares from an existing shareholder and has difficulty (or a reluctance) in going onto the share register (see Precedent 35). A transfer is incomplete until registered (*Powell v London and Provincial Bank* [1893] 2 Ch 555).

Pending registration the transferee only has an equitable title to the shares transferred to him. In general beneficial ownership passes when the transferor has done all in his power to effect a transfer, (see *Re Rose, Rose v IRC* [1952] Ch 499—but the facts must be looked at carefully; see *Dymond's Capital Taxes*, para 5.320 (FT Law & Tax). Where there is the likelihood of a company refusing or being reluctant to register a transfer the execution of a declaration of trust can produce certainty of a change in beneficial ownership (see *Macro (Ipswich) Limited* [1994] 2 BCLC 354);

2   where shares in a private company are subject to a takeover bid from a public company, thus unlocking the value of the private company shares. The shareholder may wish to transfer some shares but may be reluctant to submit the transfer with his share certificate to the company registrar at a time when this might put the shares 'in limbo' as far as acceptance of an offer is concerned. The declaration of trust (see Precedent 36) will serve the purpose of keeping the shares registered, whilst disposing of the benefit to the ultimate transferee; and

3   where there are restrictions on transfer or meetings of the board at which transfers are considered are infrequent and the proposed transferor wishes to effect a disposal before a given date or get a period of time running (appropriate for insolvency or inheritance tax purposes—see Chap 1).

It is obviously sensible that a beneficiary of a declaration of trust of shares does receive a stock transfer form duly executed by the Declarer (and the share certificate if the whole of the transferor's shareholding is involved) so that it can be presented for registration should the need or opportunity arise.

A mere entry in a share register of a transfer of shares where there has been no physical transfer document is not sufficient to effect such a transfer (see *International Credit and Investment Co (Overseas) v Adham* [1994] 1 BCLC 66).

4   Settlement provisions

So far in this chapter we have dealt with cases where shares are held absolutely for another. Settlements are a regular feature of tax planning, and shareholders may constitute themselves trustees of all or part of their shareholding by the making of a declaration of trust—their legal standing on the share register does not alter (see above, p 87) but the beneficial interest in such shares will do so.

The declaration of trust will of course set out the beneficiaries thereof and the various trust powers and provisions. For the detailed drafting of such trusts, practitioners are referred to *Practical Trust Precedents* (FT Law & Tax) and *The Encyclopaedia of Forms and Precedents* (Butterworths, 5th edn) vol 40.

A declaration of trust may be particularly appropriate in a private company with a restriction on transfers. For instance, the Articles of Association may permit transfers from a shareholder to his wife, or to himself and his spouse but otherwise require that shares to be transferred be first offered to other members. To effect a settlement, the shareholder could therefore transfer shares to himself and his wife (so that there are two trustees) and they could then make a declaration of trust in respect thereof. Precedent 37 merely illustrates what can be done by way of the recitals to a declaration of trust.

With the making of the settlement, the parties will no doubt decide whether or not to elect for hold over of any capital gain which would otherwise be realised (see Chap 1).

5 Additional matters

(a) Stamp Duty

A declaration of trust is stampable with 50p stamp duty.

(b) Registration with Inland Revenue

The declaration of trust, if signed in tandem with the creation of a settlement, should be registered with HM Inspector of Taxes.

PRECEDENTS

Precedent 33—shareholding in subsidiary held in sole name of trustee for parent company.

THIS DECLARATION OF TRUST is made this   day of   19
BETWEEN:

(1) [*registered shareholder*] of   ('the Trustee') and

(2) [*parent company*] whose registered office is situated at ('the Owner')

WHEREAS:

(A) The Owner is the beneficial owner of all the issued share capital of XYZ Limited ('the Company')

(B) The Trustee holds one share ('the Share') in the Company as nominee for the Owner

NOW THIS DEED WITNESSES:

1 The Trustee hereby DECLARES that he holds the Share UPON TRUST for the Owner absolutely

2 The Owner hereby indemnifies the Trustee against costs claims or demands in respect of the Share

IN WITNESS whereof this Deed is duly executed the day and year before written

SIGNED and delivered as a
DEED by the Trustee in
the presence of:

The Common Seal of the
Owner was hereunto affixed
in the presence of:

or

SIGNED as a DEED by XYZ Limited
by [*name*] a Director and by
[*name*] the Secretary/or a
Director:

Precedent 34—shareholding in subsidiary held in joint names of trustee and parent company.

THIS DECLARATION OF TRUST is made the   day of   19
by [name and address of Trustee Shareholder] ('the Trustee')

WHEREAS:

(A) The Trustee is the first named holder in respect of a shareholding of one £1.00 Ordinary Share in XYZ Limited ('XYZ') registered in the joint names of himself and ABC Limited ('ABC')

(B) The Trustee has at all times (as he hereby confirms) held his interest in the said Share ('the Shareholding') as a nominee of ABC

NOW IT IS HEREBY DECLARED as follows:

1 The Trustee hereby declares that he holds his interest in the Shareholding as nominee for ABC (which declaration shall extend to such further or additional Shares as the Trustee shall acquire in XYZ by reason of the Shareholding)

2 The Trustee will at the request of ABC or its successors in title attend all meetings of shareholders or otherwise of XYZ which he shall be entitled to attend by virtue of being the registered joint proprietor of the said Share or any of them and will vote at every such meeting in such manner as ABC or its successors in title shall direct and will if so required by ABC or its successors in title execute all proxies or other documents which shall be necessary or proper to enable ABC its successors in title or its nominees to vote at any such meeting in the place of the Trustee

3 The Trustee hereby authorises ABC or its successors in title to use or complete the Stock Transfer Form attached herewith (already signed by the Trustee) as ABC shall think fit and will execute such other document as may be necessary to effect the transfer of the Shareholding in such a manner as ABC or its successors in title shall direct

   IN WITNESS whereof this Deed has been duly executed the day and year before written

SIGNED and delivered as a
DEED by the Trustee in
the presence of:

Precedent 35—part shareholding held as nominee for another, nominee to vote until instructed to the contrary, indemnity to nominee

THIS DECLARATION OF TRUST made on   19
BETWEEN:
(1) [*name and address of registered holder*] ('the Nominee') and
(2) [*name and address of the underlying owner*] ('the Beneficial Owner')

WITNESSES as follows:

1 Definitions
In this Deed the following words and expressions have the following meanings:

the 'Company'	ABC Limited
the 'Shares'	100 fully paid ordinary shares of 50p each in the capital of the Company being part of the total holding of shares registered in the name of the Nominee together with any further shares stock or other securities in the Company or in any other company which are derived from or issued in right of such shares or which are distributed by the Company in respect of such shares or to which the Nominee, either alone or jointly which the Beneficial Owner, may hereafter become legally entitled by reason or as a result of the holding of such shares, including shares stock and other securities representing the same by reason of amalgamation reconstruction or re-organisation

2 Declaration of Trust
The Nominee hereby agrees and declares that he holds the Shares and all dividends interest bonuses bonus and rights issue shares and other distributions and benefits in respect thereof on trust for the Beneficial Owner

3 Dividends
The Nominee will promptly and fully account to the Beneficial Owner (or as he may direct) for all dividends distributions bonuses interest property and/or other benefits accrued or accruing upon the Shares at any time whilst they are registered in his name and the Beneficial Owner shall receive and subject thereto give a good discharge for all such dividends and other benefits

4 Voting

The Beneficial Owner agrees that until he shall give notice in writing to the Nominee to the contrary the Nominee shall be entitled to exercise all voting rights in respect of the Shares as the Nominee shall in his sole discretion decide without liability in any respect to the Beneficial Owner in consequence thereof

5 Indemnity

The Beneficial Owner will at all times indemnify and keep indemnified the Nominee and his personal representatives estate and effects against all liabilities which the Nominee may incur by reason of being the registered owner of the Shares and in particular will punctually make payment to the Nominee of any monies required in the exercise of any matters rights or benefits relating to the Shares which the Nominee or his personal representatives may be or become liable to pay together with all costs and expenses incurred by the Nominee in the execution of the trusts of this deed and any instrument of transfer in consequence thereof

6 Transfer

The Nominee will if and when requested by the Beneficial Owner certify that such instrument of transfer as is referred to above does not constitute a change in the beneficial ownership of the Shares subject to reasonable evidence being produced to him that the transfer is completed in favour of the Beneficial Owner or other nominee for the Beneficial Owner

7 Costs

The Beneficial Owner hereby agrees to pay the cost of the preparation of this Deed and all stamp duties in relation thereto

IN WITNESS whereof the parties hereto have duly executed this Deed the day and year before written

SIGNED and delivered as a
DEED by the Nominee in the
presence of:

SIGNED and delivered as a
DEED by the Beneficial Owner
in the presence of:

Precedent 36—part shareholding being the subject of an immediate gift. Private company in course of takeover.

THIS DECLARATION OF TRUST is made the   day of   19
by [name and address of registered holder] ('Mr Smith')

WHEREAS:

[Mr Smith] is desirous of gifting to his daughter [Elizabeth Smith] ('Elizabeth') the property specified in the Schedule hereto

NOW IT IS HEREBY DECLARED as follows:

1 With immediate effect [Mr Smith] DECLARES that he holds the property specified in the Schedule hereto ('the Shares') for [Elizabeth] for her own absolute use and benefit

2 [Mr Smith] will at the request of [Elizabeth] execute any Transfer or other documents as may be necessary to place the Shares in her name or as she shall direct and whilst the Shares remain registered in his own name he will vote at any shareholders meetings (in respect of the Shares) in such manner as [Elizabeth] shall direct and will if so required by [Elizabeth] execute all proxies or other documents which may or shall be necessary or proper to enable [Elizabeth] or her nominee to vote at any such meeting in the place of Mr Smith

3 [Elizabeth] has executed this document to confirm her acceptance of the gift of the Shares

IN WITNESS whereof [Mr Smith] and [Elizabeth] have duly executed this Declaration the day and year before written

THE SCHEDULE before referred to

1000 fully paid Ordinary Shares of £1.00 each in Smith (Holdings) Limited which shall include any Company succeeding to the same whether by amalgamation reconstruction takeover or re-arrangement and any Shares representing the same whether by a different capital holding in the said Company or in any other Company

SIGNED and delivered as a
DEED by [Mr Smith] in the
presence of:

SIGNED and delivered as a
DEED by [Elizabeth] in the
presence of:

Precedent 37—declaration of trust of company shares already held in the names of the trustees. Commencement and recitals only.

THIS DECLARATION OF TRUST is made the   day of   19 BY [X] and [Y] both of   [address] (hereinafter called 'the Trustees' which expression shall where the context so admits include the trustee or trustees for the time being hereof)

WHEREAS:

(A) By a transfer dated   [X] (hereinafter called 'the Settlor') transferred [100] Ordinary Shares of £1.00 each in [XYZ] Limited to the Trustees the said shareholding being designated '[AX]' Account

(B) The Trustees make this Declaration to confirm the terms upon which they have held and continue to hold such shareholding

NOW IT IS HEREBY DECLARED as follows:

1 In this deed where the context so admits

(A)   'the Trust Fund' means:
      (i)   the said [100] Ordinary Shares of £1.00 each in [XYZ] Limited designated '[AX]' Account

etc

7

Indivisible assets

1 Introduction

It may be physically impossible to divide an asset, such as a painting, and yet the owner may wish to share ownership of it with another, either for commercial reasons or to reduce a potential liability to Inheritance Tax. Where there is an asset which is indivisible, it is appropriate that such an asset is the subject of a declaration of trust where ownership is to be shared. An *inter vivos* transfer of chattels can be made either by deed or by delivery. The benefit of a transfer of ownership by deed is evidential—a declaration of trust subject to stamp duty of 50p (Stamp Act 1891, s 1 and Sched 1 as amended) will actually give evidence of the date of the transfer confirmed by the proximity of the date of the impressed stamp.

(It is not intended to deal here with the specialised area of shares in livestock (for instance a racehorse)).

Similarly, an individual may be owed a sum of money and decide to transfer part of this to another, but not wish to upset his relationship with the debtor by outwardly bringing a third party into the transaction. A declaration of trust is again therefore a suitable medium to effect what is required.

2 Declaration of trust of chattels

If an owner of chattels wishes to give an interest therein to others, whilst this can be done through the medium of a declaration of trust, the parties should be aware of some potential problems.

(a)   Reservation of benefit

It will be recalled that where after 17 March 1986 an individual disposes of any property by way of gift and either

1   possession and enjoyment of the property is not *bona fide*
    assumed by the donee at or before the beginning of the rel-
    evant period (this being the period ending on the donor's
    death and beginning seven years before that date or, if later,
    on the date of the gift), or

2   at any time in the relevant period the property is not
    enjoyed to the entire exclusion, or virtually to the entire
    exclusion of the donor, or

3   at any time the property is not enjoyed by the donee to the
    entire exclusion of the donor and of any benefit to him by
    contract or otherwise

then the property will be treated as part of the individual's estate on
his death (Finance Act 1986, s 102 and Sched 20).

In the case of property which is a chattel, retention or actual possession of the chattel is disregarded for the purposes of 2 and 3 above
if it is for full consideration in money or money's worth (Finance Act
1986, Sched 20, para 6(1)(*a*)). For example, if the donor pays the
donee market rent.

In a case where a gift of eg 50 per cent of the value of a chattel is
made, one would maintain that this is a partial gift of an asset as
opposed to a gift of an asset with a reservation (see *Commissioner
for Stamp Duties of New South Wales v Perpetual Trustee Co* [1943]
AC 425) but the possibility of 'attack' by the Revenue under the
reservation of benefit rules should not be ignored. Unfortunately,
the reservation of benefit provisions are largely based on case law
from the estate duty era and are still subject to interpretation by the
courts (see *Ingram v IRC* (1995) *The Times*, 18 May). In spite of such
uncertainty, it might be better to do something provided it has no
fiscal disadvantage, rather than do nothing at all.

If the chattel concerned is already National Heritage Property
(IHTA 1984, s 31 and FA 1985, s 95) then provided the usual under-
taking is given by the donee IHT considerations may not arise
(IHTA 1984, ss 32(5), 32A(8); FA 1985, s 95).

It should be noted that it is official practice not to treat an indemnity taken from the donee by the donor in respect of the liability to
IHT imposed on the donors personal representatives by IHTA 1984,

s 199(2) as a reservation of a benefit (see *Dymond's Capital Taxes*, para 5.441 (FT Law & Tax)).

(b)   Capital Gains Tax

A gift of chattels, or interest in them, is *prima facie* a chargeable event for capital gains tax purposes (TCGA 1992).

Works of art
Where an individual owns an asset already deemed to be of national interest and such asset is subject to an undertaking (as to viewing availability and so on) in favour of the Treasury, a gift of such asset (or part of it) will not incur liability to Capital Gains Tax provided the donee gives a similar undertaking (TCGA 1992, s 258(3)).

Other relief
There is no capital gains tax payable if a gain on the disposal of tangible moveable property amounts to £6,000 or less (TCGA 1992, s 262). Where the disposal is of an interest in such tangible moveable property, this relief is adjusted (s 262(5)). There are of course specific rules relating to the disposal of a set of items (eg chairs) to prevent relief being claimed in respect of individual items forming a set (s 262(4)).

(c)   Bills of Sale Act 1878 and Bills of Sale Act (1878) Amendment Act 1882

These Acts were designed, *inter alia*, to protect a money-lender advancing money on the security of chattels which appeared to belong to the possessor, when in fact they had already been sold to a third party or mortgaged to him. A declaration of trust by way of gift would not appear to fall within the provisions of the Acts (which would require registration as a bill of sale) (see *French v Gething* [1921] All ER 415 and *Koppel v Koppel* [1966] 2 All ER 187), but if there is to be an element of sale (albeit at an undervalue) and the chattels remain in the possession of the transferor, then it would appear that registration is necessary (see further *Fisher and Lightwood's Law of Mortgage* (10th edn, Butterworths, 1988)).

3   Declaration of trust of part of a debt

If a person owed money wishes to give that entitlement away, or sell it, he can assign the debt by a Deed of Assignment (see example in *Kelly's Draftsman* (16th edn, Butterworths)), notice to the debtor of such deed being usually given by the assignee so as to effect his title against third parties (Law of Property Act 1925, s 136). Where part of a debt is to be assigned, a declaration of trust by the person entitled to receive payment is appropriate. Such a declaration is useful where for inheritance tax reasons, for example, it is desired to give away part of a sum of money owed. This gets the seven year period running without having to wait for the receipt of the cash.

It is submitted that this will be a partial gift and that the reservation of benefit rules do not apply (see above, p 98).

4   Steps to be taken

(a)   Stamp Duty

The declaration of trust should be stamped with nominal stamp duty of 50p.

(b)   Notice

If an interest in chattels is gifted, and these are not in the possession of the donor, notice should be given to the storage firm, gallery, museum etc that the chattels should now be held on behalf of the donor and the donees.

(c)   Insurance

Similarly, insurance of the chattels the subject of the declaration of trust should be amended into the names of the donor and the donees. Payment of the premium should be shared appropriately to evidence the split in ownership.

Precedents

Precedent 38—gift of share in chattels (or proceeds of sale thereof).

THIS DECLARATION OF TRUST is made this   day of   19

BETWEEN:

(1)   ('the Donor') of   and

(2)   ('Son')   of   and   ('Daughter')   of

[   ]

WHEREAS:

(A) Following the death of [Donor's Uncle] on   19   the Donor became absolutely entitled to the picture details of which are given in the Schedule hereto ('the Picture') [subject to an Undertaking to HM Treasury in respect thereof]

(B) The Donor is proposing to sell the Picture and is in negotiation concerning such sale

[(C) On any sale of the Picture Inheritance Tax will become or will be deemed to be payable]

[(D) The picture is presently on loan at no charge to [Gallery or Museum] pending sale]

(E) The Donor is desirous of making an immediate gift of such percentage of the value of the Picture as represents one half of the proceeds of sale thereof after deduction therefrom of the costs of sale [and any IHT liability]

NOW THIS DEED WITNESSES as follows:

1 The Donor HEREBY DECLARES that henceforward she holds the Picture and the proceeds of sale thereof as Trustee UPON TRUST:

(a)   as to one half for herself

(b)   as to the other half for Son and Daughter in equal shares absolutely

SUBJECT to deducting from any proceeds of sale [any IHT liability in respect thereof and] any costs of sale of the same

2 Son and Daughter accept the gift hereby made in the shares aforesaid as their signatures hereto hereby testify

3 Son and Daughter respectively covenant to indemnify the Donor and her estate against any liability to Inheritance Tax arising by reason of the death of the Donor and in respect of the gift the subject of this deed

IN WITNESS whereof this deed has been duly executed the day and year before written

THE SCHEDULE before referred to

[Description of Picture and its present whereabouts]

SIGNED and delivered as a
DEED by the Donor in the
presence of:

SIGNED and delivered as a
DEED by Son in the presence
of:

SIGNED and delivered as a
DEED by Daughter in the
presence of:

Precedent 39—gift of share of debt owed to donor.

THIS DECLARATION OF TRUST is made this   day of   19
BETWEEN:

(1) [*name and address of donor*] ('the Donor') and

(2) [*name and address of recipient*] ('the Recipient')

WHEREAS:

(A) [*name and address of Debtor*] owes £   ('the Debt') to the Donor

(B) The Donor is desirous of giving to the Recipient entitlement to [*one half*] of the Debt ('the Assigned Part') and has agreed to make this Declaration accordingly

NOW THIS DEED WITNESSES as follows:

1 The Donor declares himself a trustee of the Assigned Part being part of the Debt and all interest due or to become due upon the Assigned Part and the full benefit and advantage of the Assigned Part in trust for the Recipient absolutely

2 The Recipient hereby covenants to indemnify the Donor and his estate against any liability to inheritance tax arising by reason of the death of the Donor in respect of the gift the subject of this Deed

IN WITNESS whereof this Deed has been duly executed the day and year before written

SIGNED and delivered as a
DEED by the Donor in the
presence of:

SIGNED and delivered as a
DEED by the Recipient
in the presence of:

8

In conjunction with wills—the half secret trust

1 Introduction

The concept of the secret or half secret trust always seemed to be the subject of a Law School lecture that would never have relevance in modern practice. This is not the case.

As a reminder:

1 the fully secret trust is just that; the will contains what appears to be an outright gift to X. To be effective as a trust, there will of course have to be communication of the trust to X and acceptance by him of the same; *Blackwell v Blackwell* [1929] AC 318 (see further *Williams on Wills* (6th edn, Butterworths) pp 368–375). Otherwise the donee is entitled to take the gift for his own benefit (*Re Stead* [1900] 1 Ch 237). It is of course vital that the testator can trust X. Such a gift covers for example a legacy for the benefit of the mistress not known to the deceased's spouse; and

2 the half secret trust; the will contains a gift to X and Y as trustees to be held upon trusts previously communicated to them (ie it is clear on the face of the will that there is a trust and that it has been accepted by the trustees).

2 The reason for a half secret trust

A will once proved becomes a document of public record. Whilst an *inter vivos* gift does not become public knowledge and is therefore the best method of keeping a gift secret, the testator may not be in a position to make such a gift during his lifetime. On death, he may wish to benefit either individuals, charities or other bodies of which his family may disapprove or which might surprise the public. Such benefits can be kept from the public gaze through the medium of the half secret trust. The will might for instance contain a gift as follows:

'I give the sum of £10,000 to X and Y as trustees to distribute the same in accordance with the provisions of a Declaration of Trust executed by them immediately prior to the execution of this my Will'.

or

'My Trustees shall transfer my Residuary Estate (as hereinbefore defined) to X and Y as trustees to hold the same in accordance with the provisions of a Declaration of Trust executed by them immediately prior to the execution of this my Will'.

Such declaration, not being a testamentary disposition, does not require to be produced for probate, so its contents remain a secret.

3   The requirements of a half secret trust

The beneficial trusts of the gift must be defined and communicated to the trustees on or before the execution of the will (*Re Bateman's Will Trusts; Brierley v Perry* [1970] 3 All ER 817) and accepted by the trustees (*Blackwell v Blackwell*, above).

The declaration cannot contain any provision for alteration or revision of the trusts (*Re Jones* [1942] Ch 323). The testator must therefore be clear prior to making his will what the beneficial interests of the half secret trust are to be. In *Re Pugh's Will Trust* [1967] 3 All ER 337 a gift 'to my trustee absolutely and I direct him to dispose of the same in accordance with any letter or memorandum which I may leave with this my Will and otherwise in such manner as he may in his absolute discretion think fit' was declared as a trust void for uncertainty as there was no letter or memoranda—the property in that case passed to the persons entitled on intestacy.

4   Enforceability of a half-secret trust

It is essential that the testator should be able to trust the trustees of the half secret trust. Unless he has communicated to the beneficiaries the fact that they are to benefit, then there is little to stop unscrupulous trustees acting in clear breach of trust and retaining the assets bequeathed to them for their own benefit. Reliable trustees and some communication to beneficiaries prior to death would appear to be sensible.

5   Inheritance Tax

On the face of it a legacy or gift of residue through the medium of a half secret trust might not appear to qualify for any exemption for Inheritance Tax purposes.

However if the underlying gift is for the benefit of an exempt person (the secret wife perhaps) or exempt institution (a registered charity or recognised political party for instance; see IHTA 1984, ss 23 and 24) then IHT relief should be available: this will of course require production of the half-secret trust document to the Capital Taxes Office (see IHTA 1984, ss 17(*b*) and 143).

6   Steps to be taken

(a)   Stamp Duty

The declaration of trust should be stamped 50p.

(b)   Safe-keeping of the declaration

If the trustees of the half secret trust are the executors of the will, then there is no objection to the declaration being lodged for safe-keeping with it. If the trustees are not the executors, then to keep the trust secret it should be kept separate from the will, and the executors left details of the whereabouts of the 'secret trustees'.

Precedent 40—declaration of trust of property to be given on half secret trust under a will.

THIS DECLARATION OF TRUST is made this   day of   19
BY X of   and Y of   ('the Trustees')

WHEREAS:

(A) JOHN SMITH of [*address*] ('the Testator') by his Will ('the Will') to be executed immediately after this Declaration has left the sum of [*£10,000*] to the Trustees to distribute the same in accordance with the provisions hereof

(B) The Trustees make this declaration to set out those provisions

NOW IT IS HEREBY DECLARED that if and when the Will becomes effective and the sum of [*£10,000*] is received by the Trustees they shall hold the same:

    (a)   as to [*£5,000*] for A absolutely

    (b)   as to [*£5,000*] for B (being the child of A) absolutely but with power to pay the same should B be a minor at the time of the Testator's death to the parent or guardian of B whose receipt shall be a good discharge.

IN WITNESS whereof this declaration has been duly executed the day and year before written

SIGNED and DELIVERED as
a DEED by X in the
presence of:

SIGNED and DELIVERED as
a DEED by Y in the
presence of:

Index

The figures in bold type refer to precedent numbers